The Star Catchers

The Star Catchers

Stories for You to Read to Your Child
To Encourage Calm, Confidence, and Creativity

Introduced by David Fontana

Story Editor: Anne Civardi

Storytellers:
Anne Civardi   Joyce Dunbar   Kate Petty   Karen Wallace

DUNCAN BAIRD PUBLISHERS

LONDON

The Star Catchers

Distributed in the USA and Canada by
Sterling Publishing Co., Inc.
387 Park Avenue South
New York, NY 10016-8810

This edition first published in the UK and USA in 2007 by
Duncan Baird Publishers Ltd
Sixth Floor, Castle House
75–76 Wells Street
London W1T 3QH
(Published in the UK as *More Nightlights*)

Managing Editor: Kelly Thompson
Editor: Ingrid Court-Jones
Managing Designer: Daniel Sturges
Designer: Justin Ford
Commissioned artwork: Franck Omer
(www.costume3pieces.com)

Library of Congress Cataloging-in-Publication Data Available

ISBN-13: 978-1-84483-407-5
ISBN-10: 1-84483-407-7
10 9 8 7 6 5 4 3 2 1

Typeset in Mrs Eaves
Color reproduction by Colourscan, Singapore
Printed in Singapore by Imago

For information about custom editions, special sales, premium and corporate purchases, please contact
Sterling Special Sales Department at 800-805-5489 or specialsales@sterlingpub.com.

A NOTE ON GENDER
In sections of this book intended for parents, "he" and "she" are used alternately, topic by topic, to
refer to the child or children, to avoid burdening the reader repeatedly with phrases such as "he or she."

C O N T E N T S

About this Book

A sequel to the much-acclaimed *Nightlights*, this collection of twenty interactive meditation stories has been specially written to calm and relax your child at bedtime, while at the same time engaging and stimulating his or her imagination.

These stories also help children in many other important ways. They help them to focus their minds and develop their powers of concentration and visualization, as well as learn more about emotions and feelings. Although not meditations in the strict sense, they do serve as a good preparation for learning real meditation later on.

Reading the stories aloud, you draw your child into wonderful adventures where he or she meets all sorts of inspiring and intriguing characters. By encouraging children to describe and elaborate on the illustrations that accompany each story, and then interact with the tale once it's under way, you can transport them into fascinating new worlds and help them to tap into their boundless creativity. These new worlds may be, in various ways, exciting, but they are also reassuring — they are safe, happy places to spend a little time.

The stories are written to appeal to girls and boys from around four to eight years old. But individual children differ greatly in their speed of development, and you are the best judge of when to read them.

Each story opens in the same way — with your child closing his eyes, picking up his magic lantern and imagining himself walking down an Enchanted Path (into the realm of dreams) with the magic lantern to light the way.

At the end of each story there's a list of positive affirmations to help draw out the story's deeper meaning. These address issues such as low self-esteem, anxiety and insecurity; gently help to instill qualities such as confidence, love, trust, courage and patience; and encourage your child to explore and understand certain situations that may arise in his or her life. A "values and issues index" is given on pages 140—4.

There's a short stretching and relaxation exercise you can do together just before you read one of the stories: see pages 24—5. And at the back of the book (pages 134—9) are some visualization exercises that will help your child on the road toward true meditation.

It's best to read the introductory sections first (pages 8—25). They discuss the needs of children and how the stories can help to address these needs. The stories themselves are best read at bedtime, when your child can relax and enjoy them to the fullest. We hope you will share his or her enjoyment, and that reading the stories together further strengthens the bonds of love and understanding between you.

A Child's Development

A happy, fulfilling childhood allows your child to develop self-esteem, self-confidence and a positive attitude – giving him the basis for becoming a happy, fulfilled adult. As he takes his first steps away from you, the loving, secure home you have provided during his early years will remain a safe haven from which he can venture out into the world alone. The benefits of such an environment are immense. Warmth and encouragement provide emotional stability, while learning and stimulation, coming from the most important people in his life, will set him on the way to a promising future.

Stimulation is partly a matter of bringing new experiences within the child's reach. It's good for a parent to concentrate on variety – a taste of what the neighbourhood, as well as your holiday spots, have to offer. But as well as actual encounters of this kind, it's beneficial to introduce a whole range of experiences mediated through the imagination. This is the role played in a child's world by model airplanes and railways, doll's houses – and, of course, the fabulous creatures often found in children's stories. Excitement, suspense, puzzlement, estrangement – even anxiety – will feature in some children's tales, extending the emotional understanding of the child while he remains safe and loved within familiar surroundings.

Being responsive to children

It's essential for your child's development that you show a special interest in what he's thinking, saying, doing or feeling. Talk with him, and listen to what he has to say, as much as possible — particularly when he needs or wants your attention. He'll enjoy, appreciate and remember the warm, cozy chats you have together. Take the chance whenever it arises (for example, straight after school) to discuss things that have happened to him during his day — you might even continue such chats at bedtime, during your storytelling session. Encourage, listen to and respond positively to your child's thoughts on people and situations, both real and imaginary. Show an interest in his play, his friends, his wishes, his anxieties. Ask him what he thinks about things — by doing so, you show that you value his opinions, which will encourage him to form and express them. When children are aware early in life that their views are prized, it helps them to develop a positive self-identity. As a bonus, if you listen to what your child has to say, he's more likely to listen to *you*!

Good stories, like those in this book, demonstrate a range of human behaviour, making it clear to the child that we aren't all the same: each individual has different concerns, different challenges to overcome. Also, life isn't static: by definition humans continually find themselves grappling with changing predicaments. Your child, inwardly and outwardly, is changing all the time. To instil the sense of our changing world through story-telling — especially when the stories deal with issues resolved and obstacles overcome — is both reassuring and deeply enlightening.

The Importance of Imagination

Imagination plays a part in almost every aspect of our lives, from everyday matters, such as giving directions, cooking a meal or choosing your clothes to activities more obviously regarded as creative, such as painting and writing. It shapes just about everything we do, making it crucial to a child's development.

Many experts on childhood now believe that pre-school training based on perception and memory — for example, teaching colours, letters and numbers — may be less important than creative play, such as dressing up, or having a make-believe tea party with teddy bears. The child psychologist Jean Piaget, who studied children at play more than fifty years ago, concluded that acting out scenarios helps them to develop a "theory of mind" — the understanding that others are different from themselves. This lays the foundations for empathy — recognizing how another person feels — which is vital for communication and relationships. Exercising their imagination at this stage will help children to practise many of the roles and skills they'll need as adults, from the ability to understand things from different perspectives to finding highly creative solutions to problems.

Narrative helps us to organize and make sense of experience: indeed, we picture our whole lives as a web of different stories. Modern visual media such as TV, films and computer

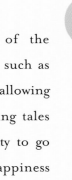

games impoverish the young by doing the work of the imagination for them. However, storytelling in books, such as this one, offers a vital corrective to this worrying trend, allowing children to construct their own pictures of the unfolding tales — their unique inner worlds. This exciting opportunity to go deeply into the mind can also bring feelings of freedom, happiness and calm — away from the stresses of real life. In addition, stories have the potential for moral guidance by showing ethical values at work in a simplified setting.

The fable tradition

The Tortoise and the Hare, Reynard the Fox and Brer Rabbit are dear to many of us. Our memories of such fables remain vivid even in adulthood — which gives some indication of the impact they have on the young mind. Animal stories present figures with which most children can affectionately identify. Yet in giving animals human traits, the stories also help to develop an understanding of human nature and behaviour, as well as teaching valuable life lessons.

The fable is often said to have begun with Aesop, around the 5th century BC. But, in fact, such narratives have more ancient roots in the literary and religious traditions of India, China and Japan.

Fables are especially effective in ethical teaching, delivering their messages more subtly and more appealingly than lectures from parents. It's easy for a child to accept that animals not only talk and wear clothes, but also have thoughts, wishes and anxieties, just like their own. More than this, the tales are child-like in their focus on the present, which makes animal fables, on the whole, easy to follow and vivid in their immediacy.

Finding Calm

The stories in this book are designed to be meditative and calming. They are not like conventional meditations, as they are full of action. However, this takes place within each story and resolves itself, in the end, into a mood of settled contentment, which will give your child peace of mind.

If she is feeling anxious, reading these stories will help to ease her troubles. She'll discover that most worries revolve around

Harmony in the home

Life is always much calmer for a child when she has warm, conflict-free relationships with those around her. As a parent, you should maintain this warmth even when you need to discipline her. Always be stern with the behaviour and not with the child: never threaten to withhold your love. If you need to warn or rebuke her, do so firmly and fairly, and in proportion to her misdemeanour rather than the inconvenience it has caused you. You could try asking her what she would propose doing to correct, or compensate for, her naughtiness. As well as being adversely affected by arguments that involve her directly, she's likely to pick up on any emotional tensions in the household. It's important to protect her from such tensions as much as possible — and be sure not to underestimate the sensitivity of your child's antennae! The calming effect of a story at bedtime can easily be undone by loud adult disagreements drifting audibly upstairs or down the hall.

things that never happen. Even situations that at first sight seem fraught with difficulty turn out to be favourable. Everything that appears worryingly strange is revealed to be unthreatening, even friendly. Lack of self-confidence is shown to be completely unfounded: we all have a far greater potential for achievement than we realize to begin with.

Children experience stress as much as adults — whether caused by bullying, performance pressures, sibling rivalry, nightmares, disappointments or quarrels. Such traumas can leave them dreading what they'll face next the day. In addition, parental controls can themselves be sources of anxiety — younger children may not understand these restraints, finding them (and their own rebellious reactions to them) confusing and frustrating. At times of worry, whatever the cause, it's important that your child can find a safe, tranquil refuge within her own mind.

The stories in this book help your child to discover such a sanctuary. Encourage her to choose a setting from one of the tales — for example, the garden in "The Red Trumpet Flowers", or the field of buttercups in "The Magic Meadow" — and to imagine herself going there and exploring all the beautiful things she sees around her. Explain to her that once she has created this space in her mind, she can go there at any time, whenever she needs to calm down. The knowledge that she has her own unique haven will help her to realize that peace and happiness can come from within herself, as well as from being valued and loved by others.

Gaining Confidence

Children are not born with a sense of who or what they are — indeed, they don't perceive themselves as even being separate from their mothers until their second year. After reaching the milestone of self-awareness, they gradually build up a self-identity — a picture of themselves formed from what adults tell them and the experiences they have in their lives. Once they've formed this picture, they start to evaluate their competence and worth, and their assessment of these qualities gives them their level of self-esteem.

Simply by spending time reading the stories in this book to your child, you're letting him know that you enjoy and value his company. This endorsement in itself will boost his self-worth, giving him the confidence to be more open in discussing his concerns and worries with you. Some of the stories are specifically intended to help your child gain a true sense of self — in "A Sheep's Best Song", for example, he'll learn that he should value his own talents, rather than try to be like his friends. Other stories will help him to understand other people's emotions, which will improve his social skills — again building his self-esteem and self-confidence.

Moreover, storytelling helps a child's confidence by extending the range of his imagination. It's almost as if each story were a distant land that the child feels proud to have visited, and

14

"captured" in his memory. The expansion of a child's repertoire of favourite stories is also an extension of his inner boundaries — the limits of his imagination.

Increased confidence, and the greater independence that comes with it, in turn encourage better interactions with others, including a more rewarding contribution to group activities. The result is a virtuous circle, because the capacity for making friends more easily gives a further boost to confidence, ensuring that successful friendships become even more likely.

Feeling at home with language

The best way to increase your child's vocabulary and understanding of language is to talk with him, from babyhood on, about everything you see and do together. Read aloud from baby books as soon as he can sit up. In this way, your child will be introduced to the pleasures of language from the very start. Graduate to stories when he's old enough, and as you're reading, pause briefly to explain any words that he doesn't understand.

Some time between the ages of 4 and 7, you'll probably notice your child getting really interested in words, and starting to play with them, and even make jokes with them. Encourage this, and make jokes together. If you relish words (and rhymes) with him, and combine this with explaining the meanings of words, and examples of how they're used, you'll be contributing hugely to building his language skills and vocabulary. At 5, a child might have a spoken vocabulary of around 5,000 words; by the age of 6, 8,000 to 14,000 words is usual.

The Power of Stories

The best stories speak to us of universal aspects of our common humanity — our life experiences, our emotions, our hopes and fears, and the various ways in which we respond to the circumstances that occur. Often, the characters are thoroughly representative, while stopping short of being allegorical. Although there will be a particular setting, and ideally one that is vividly realized, the essence of the story will transcend this, dramatizing situations that we find familiar.

Visualization

Storytelling shares a strong emphasis on the visual with certain forms of meditation. For example, as soon as the word "wood" is mentioned, an image is conjured up in the mind's eye. Good stories build on this image to fill in more detail, yet without allowing the setting to overwhelm the action. "It's windy in the wood, and autumn leaves are blowing all over the place." This is enough to set the scene. A confident writer of stories for children knows how much to leave to their imagination. A few choice words, without too many adjectives, will summon up vivid mental pictures, whereas if the story piles on too many descriptive details, the effect will be distracting, and therefore counter-productive.

By all means ask your child to tell you more about the scene they've imagined, but avoid elaborating it too much yourself. Have faith in their powers of visualization. Let simple words in simple combinations work their magic.

When a child enters the world of a story, the encounter can be a profound one. Good stories not only capture the imagination, they send it in exciting new directions — yet never into a realm that is wholly unreal. Beneath the fanciful surface of a story about animals, exotic lands or magical transformations there may be a core of universal truth that your child assimilates. The momentum of the narrative and the vividly realized details of the setting draw her in to situations that are essentially emotional. She reacts with empathy and her capacity for compassion and intuitive understanding is extended.

A child enjoys many aspects of storytelling simultaneously — meeting new characters, going to new places (even different planets), finding unexpected magic, and being soothed, even in passages that may excite vicarious anxiety, by the storyteller's familiar and reassuring voice. The resolution, if a happy one (as it is in all twenty stories here), defuses all tensions, leaving the child with a sense of having been on a real adventure — and the parent with the knowledge that a small piece of wisdom has been taken painlessly to heart.

By interacting with the stories, your child is unwittingly learning lessons from them. When she has her own emotional lows, such as anxiety, fear, frustration, disappointment or anger, she can draw on what she has absorbed. The characters' experiences may help her to understand the way she is feeling, and to realize that others have had those feelings, too.

Reading to Children

As the storyteller, you are in a position to greatly influence how your child receives your story. Don't think of yourself merely as a mouthpiece and a spectator: instead, be mindful of the fact that your role is a more complex one in which you not only take on the role of actor, but also of conjurer — not to mention, of course, the role of devoted parent showing infinite patience, love and support.

It's best to throw yourself wholeheartedly into the tale — any reservations you have, or any distractions you are entertaining at the back of your mind, would be picked up instantly by super-sensitive radar. Show that you have complete belief in the story as it unfolds. Your enthusiasm and depth of involvement will be apparent in the tone of your voice, the rhythm of your speech, your characterizations and your facial expressions as you share your child's reactions, whether surprise, excitement, or sympathy. Many adults find that they rediscover the wonders of childhood themselves while reading to their children, as they see the world through a child's eyes again.

It's important not to rush the stories. Speak slowly, allowing the music of the words to have their spellbinding effect. Gradually build up the atmosphere, pausing a little now and then to let your child picture the scenes vividly in his mind. Gently draw his attention to anything he may have missed — perhaps by adding a little improvisation of your own. Make sure that you allow plenty of time for relaxed discussion afterwards, if your child isn't too tired, before lights out.

In such conversations use language that your child can understand easily, and avoid talking down to him, or letting him think that you that are trying to test his knowledge. When you share your own reactions to the story, take care that you don't dominate his imaginative thinking. To tease out his own responses, you can ask questions, such as "I wonder why … ?" — as if there's something that you don't understand and would like explained. Make a point of praising his responses, perhaps with something along the lines of, "I hadn't thought of it that way." This will show that you value his opinion, and will encourage him to share his thoughts again in future.

When your child is exposed to inspiring stories, his own creativity is stimulated, perhaps prompting him to improvize stories of his own. You can use the stories in this book as a starting point for all kinds of imaginative explorations. Try investigating alternative scenarios together, using a cue such as, "What do you think would happen if … ?" Try talking about the pictures as well as the stories. Ask him what he thinks might happen if one or more of the characters from one story were to meet characters from another story. You may make some interesting discoveries.

The Art of Concentration

Concentration is essential for learning — for reading or listening properly and for absorbing information. One of the most common challenges that parents face is to get their child to focus on the task in hand. The child's difficulty is to clear everything else out of her head when there are so many distractions buzzing around. Combined with this is the problem of surplus energy: it may not seem natural to a child even to sit still, never mind concentrate. Restlessness is as much a defining feature of childhood as playfulness or experimentation.

After a long, full day, tiredness does not necessarily make things any easier. All parents know the irritability that can come with extreme fatigue — though this is more likely to manifest itself in company, when there are more stimuli than the child can cope with. At bedtime there will inevitably be a letting go. Now's the time to soothe your child with a story and ease the transition from daytime activity to nighttime repose. Preparations for bed will help to foster a mood of relaxation, leading to calm. Your priority now is to smoothe away cares and show your affection and support. This is mainly self-fulfilling: if you feel loving toward your child, it will show in your tone of voice. Avoid referring to anything controversial or fraught with anxieties.

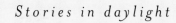

Stories in daylight

While the stories in this book are intended mainly for reading at bedtime, they can just as easily be read during the day — perhaps to restore calm after a period of intense activity, or to help your child to deal with a particular problem in her life, or as part of her language learning. Encourage older children to read the stories quietly by themselves or out loud to you. They may also enjoy writing stories, poems or short plays based on themes covered in this book.

When your child feels the need for something more physical than reading, you could easily devise some activities using her favourite stories as a starting point. She could draw, paint or make collages of some of the characters, or act out scenes using dolls, soft toys or puppets. Alternatively, she could dress up and act out a scene with a friend, or put on a play, creating magical costumes and scenery from everyday items. Imaginative activities of this kind will develop your child's creativity and inventiveness, boost their self-confidence and help them to learn.

The combination of a relaxed atmosphere, an intimate setting and a young mind that has let go of daytime excitements is ideal for nurturing the concentration required to appreciate a story. The way in which the stories in this book involve the child as one of the central characters will help to focus her attention. Soon she'll be thoroughly absorbed in the fictional world to which you've transported her — at ease and at peace, concentrating fully, and using her imagination freely. You're privileged to witness this — so value and enjoy!

Affirmations

When we view our lives optimistically, we can alter our own perception of our daily experiences. It's all too easy for us to focus on what's wrong, or to always want something other than what we already have. But this is a recipe for discontent and anxiety. Better to value ourselves and our relationships by counting our blessings and living by what we believe in. Most probably, we're living in privileged times, in an affluent part of the world, where excellent medical care is available to cure even serious sickness, or, at the very least, to ease it. We have every reason to be positive.

From a very early age, children can begin to pick up the habit of negative thinking from those around them. The best way to help your child to become a positive thinker is to become one yourself. Replace negative habits with positive ones. Stop expecting things to go wrong, and vow to do the best you can with what's available. Make it a daily habit to think with gratitude of the people you love and all the other good things in your life. Positive thinking of this kind brings contentment and inner calm.

To encourage your child to focus on the positive, each story in this book ends with a list of affirmations designed to draw out the story's deeper meanings — that is, the values and virtues it embodies. When you've finished reading a story, it's a good idea to discuss these affirmations with your child (so long as he isn't

22

too tired) and talk about how they relate to the narrative. Encourage him to add his own interpretations, using indirect questions to prompt his responses, such as "I wonder why … ?" rather than "Why do you think … ?" This approach will remove any pressure from your child to find the "correct" answer, because he'll realize that you're thinking about the stories, too. Don't forget to praise his responses — children derive great pleasure and a good deal of self-confidence from the knowledge that their own opinion has helped an adult to understand something.

Ending the day on a positive note

As well as reading a story to your child at bedtime, spend some quiet time discussing things that have happened during his day. Concentrate on the most positive events and the good things that he, or people who are important to him, managed to achieve that day.

Then, together, plan at least one positive activity — no matter how small — for your child to do the following day. Perhaps he could do something he really enjoys or help someone out with a task. End the day on an optimistic note by encouraging him to go to sleep with happy thoughts about the things he plans to do. This will help him to sleep well and avoid nightmares.

You could even devise an affirmation together for him to recite — say, three times before he goes to sleep and/or three times in the morning to get his day off to a good start. When you regularly affirm the positive, optimistic feelings tend to stick around.

A Way to Begin

Before you start to read one of the stories in this book, or any other bedtime story, you might like to do this short, simple stretching and relaxation exercise with your child. This could become part of the routine you share together every night. Most children really enjoy this kind of gentle, quiet exercise, and it's a good way to get them to relax, calm down and burn off any excess energy at the end of a busy day. By helping your child to relax her body, you help her to relax her mind, too. This makes it easier for her to empty her head of thoughts and concentrate on the story that you're about to read.

First, ask your child to lie on her bed, or on the floor with her head on a cushion. Ask her to put her hands on her tummy and imagine there's a big balloon inside it. Now, in a calm, soft voice, say to her:

"Gently close your eyes.
Breathe in slowly and deeply through your nose and
let the big balloon inside your tummy slowly fill up.
Now breathe out as slowly as you can through your
nose and let the balloon become smaller and smaller until
there's no air left in your tummy at all."

24

Ask her to do four more breaths like this, and then say:

"Now squeeze your hands into a tiny ball, as small and
tight as you can. Open them slowly and stretch them out as big
and wide as you can — as big as the biggest giant's hands.
Give them a little shake. Let your hands and arms
feel floppy and relaxed."

"Now squeeze your toes tight. Curl them up as small as you
can. Uncurl them and stretch them out as big and wide as you
can — as wide as the biggest giant's feet. Give them a shake.
Let your feet and legs feel floppy and relaxed."

"Now scrunch your eyes, forehead, eyebrows, nose and
mouth so that your face is as wrinkled as a little old elf. Relax
your face and let the back of your head sink into the cushion."

"Notice how relaxed and floppy your whole body is.
Now imagine it feels warm and toasty, and a lovely warm
feeling is moving up your legs, your tummy, your
chest, your arms, your neck, to your head."

"Now relax your mind. Is it ready to listen? To listen
to the story you're about to be told? I think it is!"

The Helpful Fox

Close your eyes and think about all the kind people who help us when we're sick or hurt or lost. You'd always help someone out if you could, wouldn't you? How would that feel? Let's see if you can find out! Pick up your magic lantern and walk down the Enchanted Path. Where will it lead you tonight?

You're strolling down a hill toward a little glade of trees. The sun has just risen and the grass around you still glistens and sparkles with dew. You can hear the splashing sound of a distant stream rushing along the bottom of the valley. As you tramp down toward the glade, you hear the sound of muffled voices coming from among the trees. What can be down there, you wonder, as you quicken your pace?

But wait! Someone is panting down the hill behind you. "Is this the way to the hospital?" asks a rather gruff voice, and you turn around to see a very strange sight.

27

A small golden rabbit is being carried on the back of the fox who has asked you the question.

"Don't you normally chase and eat rabbits?" you ask the fox, sounding most surprised.

"Not this one," says the fox. "She let one of my cubs stay warm in her burrow when he'd wandered too far from our den. And now she's got a big thorn in her paw and I want to find her a doctor."

Well, this all seems very odd, but you want to help the fox and the rabbit. So you tell them about the voices you heard coming from the glade down below.

"Ah, that must be the hospital," says the fox, and off he marches, with you following close behind.

When you arrive at the hospital, what a sight greets your eyes! You can see a number of animals lying in leafy hammocks slung between the trees, or resting on beds of soft grass — there's a cat with its paw in a splint next to a pigeon with its wing in a sling.

At first, the hospital looks rather disorganized to you, but soon you spot an owl sitting at a log desk.

One by one, he hoots out the name of a patient and asks him or her to come up and sign in.

Now a flurry of activity in a hollow tree trunk catches your eye. A family of mice are pounding red berries, flower petals and herbs with a large stone. As you watch, another mouse carefully tips the fine powder they have made into half an eggshell and mixes it with drops of water to make a smooth potion.

The owl hoots out to you, "Please take a seat in the waiting room. Dr Rooster will arrive soon."

You sit down next to a dog who whispers to you in a croaky voice that he's lost his bark. On your other side there's a little green frog who seems to have lost her leap. Just then, an eagle glides down from the sky, and guess what's clinging to his back? It's a furry brown bat.

"She keeps on flying into things and bumping her head," the kind eagle explains. "I'm hoping the doctor can help her to find her way in the dark again."

29

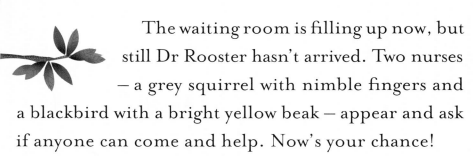

The waiting room is filling up now, but still Dr Rooster hasn't arrived. Two nurses — a grey squirrel with nimble fingers and a blackbird with a bright yellow beak — appear and ask if anyone can come and help. Now's your chance!

You follow the two nurses into the surgery and there you help to bathe wounds, bandage the leg of the frog and give throat medicine to the dog. When the rabbit is brought in, you hold her paw steady while Nurse Blackbird picks out the thorn with his sharp yellow beak. Then you gently dab the wound with the soothing potion that the mice have created.

You're feeling a little tired after all your hard work, but now's not the time to rest. Four squirrels rush in carrying a stretcher woven from twigs. Lying on top and writhing quite violently is a long black snake who's tied up in the tightest of knots! This is an emergency! The nurses scratch their heads.

"I wish Dr Rooster were here," says Squirrel. "With his strong feet, he could easily untie this poor snake."

"I can help!" you shout enthusiastically, stroking the snake's scaly skin to calm it down, even though you don't feel very brave. What if the snake bites you?

You take a deep breath. The other animals look on nervously as you grasp the snake's tail and carefully, very carefully, untie the tight knot.

Phew! You've cured the snake and he's very grateful. So are the nurses. And so is Dr Rooster, who's just arrived. But, after all the excitement, you feel very sleepy. The helpful fox takes hold of your arm and leads you back home the way you first came.

What a long day it's been. You're glad you were brave enough to help, but now it's time to shut your eyes and dream about the animal hospital in the little glade of trees, and about all your new friends — the ones who were hurt, the ones you have helped.

Affirmations

- Always treat people the way you would like them to treat you.
- You can get a great deal of pleasure from helping someone, especially if it makes him or her feel better.
- There are helpful things you can do that others might not be able to do as well as you.
- Situations that appear to be scary at first often turn out to be less frightening than you imagined.
- It's important to stay calm and keep a clear head in an emergency. Then you'll be able to help as much as you can.

The Star
Catchers

Close your eyes and think about the stars that twinkle so high up in the clear night sky. What makes them sparkle and burn so brightly? Imagine if you could reach up and catch one. What might you do with it? Let's see if you can find out! Pick up your magic lantern and walk down the Enchanted Path. Where will it lead you tonight?

You find yourself in a forest of silver trees on a faraway planet. It's a velvety, purple night and among the moonlit trees you see two children walking toward you. Both are wearing shimmering silk robes that flow gently behind them. Between them, they carry a net made of silver string fastened to the end of a pure white pole. Inside the net, tiny lights seem to glow.

The boy and girl stop and smile at you. "Welcome," says the girl. "I'm Princess Galaxy and this is my brother, Prince Comet. Who are you?"

You've never met a prince or princess before, but they seem friendly, so you tell them your name. Then you ask them about the lights inside their net.

"This is stardust," replies Princess Galaxy. "But we're hoping to catch a really special star tonight as a present for our mother, Queen Andromeda."

"She'll put the star on her crown to make it sparkle extra brightly at the palace ball tonight," adds Prince Comet.

"Is it easy to catch a star?" you ask Princess Galaxy excitedly. "I'd like to catch one too." But the prince and princess shake their heads.

"It's a very difficult thing to do," replies Princess Galaxy, softly. "First, we have to be lucky enough to see one falling through the sky."

"Then we have to be as fast as arrows and scoop it up in our net before it tumbles to earth and loses its starshine," adds the prince.

You listen very quietly and nod your head. But you know that even though stars sometimes appear to be near, they're really a long, long way away. How can the prince and princess possibly catch one in their net?

But before you have time to ask, something extraordinary happens.

The prince and princess hold out their arms and you watch in amazement as two delicate pairs of glimmering wings unfold from beneath their silk robes. Up, up they soar into the night sky until they are two tiny specks of light high above your head. Now you have the answer to your question.

The prince and princess can fly!

You watch as they dip and weave in the purple sky. It's almost as if they're chasing something. But what can it be? Then suddenly you see it! A brilliant star is falling toward the ground in a great sparkling arc.

You gaze as the princess swoops down with the net to catch the star. But she misses it! Then the prince zooms downward and takes hold of the net. Your heart is hammering in your chest. Any minute now, he's bound to crash into the ground. But no! Just in time, he scoops up the star in the magic silver net and flies upward to join his sister.

Now the prince and princess are circling high above you. A minute later, they land softly by your side.

"This is the very biggest star I've ever caught," whoops Prince Comet with a huge grin on his face. "Mother will be so pleased with me."

You walk with the prince and princess to their palace. On the way, they explain that they've been out for a long time and they don't want their mother, Queen Andromeda, to worry. When they lead you into the great hall, you see her sitting on a shiny silver throne and you know she's been waiting anxiously. In her hands, she's holding a glittering crown made of gold. You stand with Princess Galaxy as her brother presents his mother with his magnificent star.

The Queen is delighted and immediately places the sparkling star in the centre of her golden crown. Then she kisses Prince Comet three times on each cheek to show how much she loves the gift.

You notice that the Queen seems to have forgotten all about her daughter, Princess Galaxy. You ask the princess if she minds that her mother is so pleased with her brother and hasn't yet turned to greet her.

"Oh, no, I don't mind about that at all," she replies.

"To see a falling star is hard enough, but to catch one that's so big and brilliant is almost impossible."

Now Princess Galaxy takes your hand and smiles at you. "My brother has earned my mother's kisses," she says. "And I'm glad for him."

You look into the Princess's eyes and sense the kindness flowing through her fingertips. In that very moment, you feel as if you're soaring up through the velvety sky yourself, as free as a bird, as fast as an arrow and surrounded by twinkling stars. Perhaps, one day, you too will catch your own shooting star, big and bright enough to decorate a queen's golden crown. You never know, do you?

Affirmations

- Let others enjoy their well-earned praise. It's only fair that special effort should be recognized and rewarded.
- If you feel good about yourself and believe in yourself, you won't feel jealous or envious of other people's achievements.
- If you can step back and happily watch others receive the attention they deserve, you will find it easier to step up and take the glory when your turn comes.
- Try to understand how other people feel when they achieve something special, even if they seem to forget you're around.

Home to
Penguin Island

Close your eyes and imagine you're standing on a stony beach by a cold grey sea. Your clothes are thick and woolly, so you're feeling snug and warm. All around, you can hear strange barking noises, but the mist hanging in the air makes it tricky to see. What could these noises be? Let's see if you can find out! Pick up your magic lantern and walk down the Enchanted Path. Where will it lead you tonight?

You're on Seal Island, and everywhere you look there are seals basking in the pale sun. As the mist lifts, you glimpse another island, far across the water. The sound of squawking penguins drifts toward you — that must be Penguin Island. Just then, a baby penguin shuffles up to you, looking sad and lost and lonely. You realize she's the only penguin on Seal Island. But how can that be?

38

She must have been washed off Penguin Island, away from her mother, and been carried here across the sea. You can see that she's too young to swim back alone and you want to help the little penguin, but how?

As you walk along the beach trying to think of a way, you spot a huge mother seal down by the water's edge. She's barking and standing up on her flippers as if she's searching for something. You're frightened and run back up the beach, where thistly bushes grow in the sand. Suddenly, the baby penguin squawks loudly. She seems to be looking at a particular bush. When you lift up the branches, you find a tiny seal hiding underneath. Just like the little penguin, he's lost his way in the mist and has been parted from his mother.

Carefully, you pick up the seal pup and carry him toward the other seals by the ocean. Feeling braver, he gives a little bark. The mother seal hears and roars in reply. Now you realize that it's *her* baby you've rescued.

When you're close to the mother seal, you put her baby down. The mother wriggles up to him and sniffs him all over. Then she looks up and gives you a grateful smile. She seems to be asking if there's anything she can do in return.

40

At that moment, a bright idea pops into your head. You go as near as you dare to the big mother seal and point to Penguin Island. She looks at you, then at Penguin Island, then at the sad little penguin who has followed behind you. Now she understands what it is you'd like her to do — you want her to take the penguin home to his mother. She lies down and the baby penguin hops on to her head. You sit on the sand with the seal pup and, together, you watch as his mother streaks through the water. It's still very cold, but you feel warm and happy to have helped the little penguin find her way home.

Affirmations

- If you are kind or helpful to other people, they are likely to be kind or helpful in return.
- If you help to solve a problem for someone else, it makes you feel good about yourself.
- Let others help you when things get difficult. Trusting someone else often makes it easier to work out how to overcome difficult or scary situations.
- Remember that there's always a way to communicate with others, even if you don't speak the same language.

A Sheep's Best Song

Close your eyes and imagine you're weaving your way through a meadow of soft grass and bright yellow dandelions. Ahead of you is a big red barn, and from beyond it come the sounds of a farmyard. Cows, horses and chickens are all making excited noises. What's going on? Let's see if you can find out! Pick up your magic lantern and walk down the Enchanted Path. Where will it lead you tonight?

As you head toward the barn, you pass a large vegetable garden. Rows of bean plants with their brilliant red flowers curl up thin poles stuck into the earth. Carrots with feathery tops grow beside pea plants covered in small white blossoms. A large pink pig is hoeing between the rows to keep down the weeds. As he pushes his hoe through the rich brown soil, you hear him singing a song.

43

"Oink, oink, oink," goes the merry pig, tapping his foot as he sings. He's so busy singing he doesn't even realize you're there.

At the edge of the vegetable garden a duck quacks happily to herself as she nibbles the long grass.

At that moment, the pig looks up and notices you. "You're just in time to see the show," he exclaims.

"What show?" you ask curiously.

"The Animal Talent Competition, of course!" cries the pig. "It's in the farmyard. Hurry! All the animals are waiting patiently for you!"

How can they be waiting for you, you wonder? You want to ask the pig, but there's no time for questions.

You follow the pig around the side of the barn and arrive in a farmyard, full of cows and horses, goats and chickens, sheep and geese, pigs and ducks. The air is buzzing with excitement and anticipation. Some animals have garlands of flowers around their necks. Others have them on top of their heads.

Now you spot a stage made from a big wooden cart at one end of the farmyard. It's decorated with red and blue streamers, flowers and bunches of brightly coloured balloons that float in the breeze.

In front of the cart, hay bales are set out for the audience to sit on. There's one big bale that seems to be especially for you, so you quickly sit down and wait for the show to begin.

Just then, a black and white sheep dog jumps on to the stage. "Animals and our special friend," he barks, bowing toward you. "Welcome to the Animal Talent Competition! Our first act is a dance."

You sit back and watch a rooster dance with a red hen. They take two steps forward and one step back. The rooster crows and the hen fluffs out her wings.

You clap your hands delightedly. It's a lovely, dainty dance — just the sort a rooster and hen might do.

Next comes a big carthorse who clip-clops around the stage doing his own special tap dance. Then a gaggle of geese follow one behind the other in a perfect figure of eight, without making any mistakes at all.

"Please welcome the pig," cries the sheep dog, and you watch as the pig rolls around in a pile of thick mud and turns himself completely brown. You laugh loudly as you clap your hands together. It's exactly what a pig would do!

More acts follow until the last animal, a pretty white sheep, climbs on to the stage.

She bows politely and then pulls three big red tomatoes from behind her floppy ears.

All the animals are silent. What on earth is going on? Everyone knows sheep don't keep tomatoes behind their ears! Then the sheep throws the tomatoes in the air and suddenly you understand. She's trying to juggle with them! But all three tomatoes drop on to the ground – splat! splat! splat! It's obvious that the sheep doesn't know how to juggle at all.

It's a disaster! The other farm animals start to boo at the poor white sheep. Then, all together, they turn toward you, and you realize that somehow you must save the show.

Jumping down from your hay bale, you run on to the stage. It's clear that the sheep needs your help badly.

"Sing 'baa' like a sheep," you whisper into her right ear, gently patting her soft shoulder. Then, straight away, you turn to face the farm animals and open your arms wide.

46

"Animals, great and small," you announce loudly. "Please give a warm welcome for a magnificent sheep with a very special song."

Now you sit back on your hay bale and wait with your heart racing in your chest as the sheep begins her best song. At first the "baa" is so soft you can barely hear it at all. Then it becomes bolder, louder and louder. Finally it fills the air, soaring over the farmyard and into the meadow. All the animals clap and cheer — the sheep's song has filled them with joy. You're happy too. But best of all, the sheep's overjoyed when she wins the competition — all because she did exactly what a sheep would do!

Affirmations

- Be pleased with the things you do well, even if you think they're not as good as the things other people can do.
- Always do the things you know you are capable of doing. So long as you try your best, people will be proud of you — and you will be proud of yourself.
- If you see someone doing something a little foolish, be kind. One day that someone could be you!
- Be generous with your praise. A few words of kindness and support can make people feel happier and more confident.

The Shadow Child

Close your eyes and think about shadows. What makes a shadow? The light of course. What can chase away shadows? The light of course. Do shadows have a life of their own? Let's see if you can find out! Pick up your magic lantern and walk down the Enchanted Path. Where will it lead you tonight?

You're in the garden of a city square. It's a shadow garden. There are shadow flowers, some nodding, others tall and straight. There's a shadow fountain gushing over a shadow pool full of shadow fish. There are shadow mothers with their shadow babies. There's an old shadow man feeding shadow birds. And there's you.

Beside you is *your* shadow. Is it the sun shining high up in the sky that's

49

making your shadow? Or is it your magic lantern? You're not sure. But your shadow is there on the path, quite clear for you to see. It moves when you move. It stays still when you're still.

You're puzzled by this shadow garden. You want to make it real. But how? Maybe your shadow can do this for you. But no, it only does the things you do. You'd like a shadow that can do things all by itself.

You make movements for a while, watching your shadow move, too. You jump on your shadow. Your shadow jumps, too. You turn from your shadow and try to run away. Your shadow follows you. You laugh, point, skip and shout. Your shadow follows every movement, but makes no noise.

Now you have a mischievous thought. Perhaps you can escape from your shadow. You start to do cartwheels. Round and round, over and over. Then, suddenly you stop. Amazingly, it's worked — your shadow moves on and spins away all alone. It waves cheekily at you. Your shadow seems to have a mind of its own. But how?

Maybe it's not your shadow. Is it someone else's? You check your own shadow, the one that does exactly as you do. But it's no longer at

your feet. It's over there — dancing, skipping and pointing. You know it's your shadow because it has your shape. Whatever will it do next?

You watch as it runs on to a flower bed and starts to naughtily pick off the shadow flower heads, one by one.

"Who did that?" says a voice.

"Not me," you answer. "The Shadow Child did it."

Now the Shadow Child jumps into the shadow fountain, startling the shadow fish, and begins to splash shadow people as they pass by.

"Who's doing that?" says a voice.

"Not me," you answer. "The Shadow Child did it."

Oh dear. What now? The Shadow Child snatches a shadow toy from a shadow baby and runs away with it. You can see that the shadow baby is most upset.

"Who snatched the baby's toy?" says a voice.

"Not me," you answer. "The Shadow Child did it."

Then the Shadow Child creeps up to the shadow man who's feeding bread to the shadow birds. It darts among them, scattering them into the air.

"Who did that?" says a voice.

"Not me," you say at once. "No, it really wasn't me. The Shadow Child did it."

The Shadow Child carries on behaving wildly. It kicks a shadow ball and pulls a shadow dog's tail.

"Who's doing this?" says an angry voice.

"Not me," you answer. "The Shadow Child did it."

"But everyone knows that their shadow is a part of themselves. The Shadow Child is *your* shadow so it's a part of you. It can only do what you do," replies the voice. "And you're scaring the birds, the fish, the dog and the babies. That's not a very kind thing to do."

You think about what the voice has just told you. Now you understand that, whether you like it or not, the Shadow Child does indeed belong to you. You, and only you, have the power to stop it from getting up to any more mischief.

As soon as you realize this, the Shadow Child stops running and stands completely still. Suddenly, there it is — your own shadow, doing just what you're doing. Because you have accepted that the naughty shadow is part of you — that it's your responsibility — it has come back to you, its owner, and is calm and still.

And in that moment the garden becomes full of colour. It's real. You can see lots of beautiful pink and white flowers nodding in the sunlight. You

52

can see the sparkling fountain and the red and gold fishes. You can see a laughing baby with his fluffy, blue toy, and a stooped old man feeding bread to some small speckled sparrows.

You feel thankful. Peace has returned to the garden. You and your shadow are one again. It can do nothing without your agreement, nothing you don't do first.

What a comforting thought that is. Now you feel calm and ready to rest. You know that shadows, no matter how mysterious they are, have no life of their own. They're just a creation of the light, the light that's in the magic lantern you're holding. Now, when you put it down, all the shadows fade away.

Affirmations

- Everybody has a shadow. We also have a shadow self that sometimes does things we wouldn't do. It's important never to pretend that this shadow self is not you. If you blame others you take away your power to put things right.
- It's best to own up to any naughty things you do and to be ready to face the consequences. If you do this, you can trust yourself and other people can trust you, too. This is called responsibility.
- When you take responsibility you're more in charge of your life. You can make it as good as you want it to be.

An Alligator's
Good Friends

Close your eyes and imagine you're standing by a swamp, surrounded by tall, spiky grass. The air is hot and steamy, which makes your clothes so damp that they cling to your skin. As you stand sweltering in the heat, you spot something that looks like a big green plate wobbling in the water in front of you. What can it be? Let's see if you can find out! Pick up your magic lantern and walk down the Enchanted Path. Where will it lead you tonight?

You weave your way through the grass until you reach the fringes of the swamp. The water here has an earthy smell, almost like mud. Now that you're closer, you realize that the wobbly green plate is a big lily pad. But still you wonder what's making it move. Then you see the shiny green back of a turtle slide off it and plop into the water.

You watch a little frog leap from one leaf to the next. A snail crawls lazily up to meet him, while a dragonfly with glittering, silvery wings glides back and forth above their heads.

Suddenly, something stirs in the swamp, and you notice two golden eyes that seem to float above the water. Then you see a long, bumpy snout and a mouth full of razor-sharp teeth. It's an alligator.

You watch, a little afraid, as the alligator swims close to the shore. A long-legged heron wades into the water, keeping a watchful eye on the reptile.

Just then, the alligator opens his huge mouth and two little birds jump inside. All at once, they begin to peck at the alligator's sharp, pointy teeth.

"Watch out birds!" you cry, jumping up and down and clapping your hands. "The alligator will eat you!"

The birds flutter nervously away at the loud noise. Now the heron sweeps up to you. "You shouldn't have done that," she says sternly. "Those little birds are the alligator's friends. They keep his teeth clean and healthy by eating pieces of leftover food. And, because the alligator knows this, he'll never hurt them."

Even though you were trying to help, you're upset and embarrassed. Now the little birds may go hungry and the alligator will have dirty teeth.

"How can I make things better?" you ask the heron.

"If you stay quiet and still, the birds won't be scared and they'll return," replies the heron.

Sure enough, the brave little birds soon hop back inside the alligator's mouth and carry on pecking between the rows of his sharp teeth.

Now you understand the friendship between the alligator and the birds, and you're delighted. A smile spreads across your face as you sit back and bask in the hot, steamy sunshine, just like the contented alligator.

Affirmations

- It's best not to interfere too much in other people's lives. Situations that appear to be wrong, worrying or frightening to you, often turn out to be quite all right.
- If at first you don't understand something, be patient. The answer will usually become clear with time.
- Try to understand a new situation before making up your mind what to do. Then you won't make the wrong decision.
- People, animals and plants help each other in all sorts of ways. It's good to help others in any way you can, too.

The Lovable
Monster

Close your eyes and imagine you're picking fruit in a grove of leafy banana trees. As you peel the skin from a large, ripe, yellow banana, the ground beneath you begins to rumble and shudder. It's as if something huge and heavy is coming toward you. But who or what can it be? Let's see if you can find out! Pick up your magic lantern and walk down the Enchanted Path. Where will it lead you tonight?

Cautiously, you peep out from under a tree and there, walking down a dusty road beside the grove, is a huge, hairy figure, unlike anyone you've ever seen before. As he lumbers along, he stops to sniff flowers, to chew leaves, to nibble mushrooms. You watch as he bangs two sticks together. He stops and listens; he seems to like the sound the sticks make, and he's so busy listening to them that he doesn't look where he's going.

Suddenly, the ground appears to swallow him up. You edge nearer to the spot where he disappeared and see that he's fallen into a deep, dark pit that had been hidden by lots of thick, leafy branches.

Just then, out of the bushes all around, some people from a nearby village come running. They gather around the pit, shouting, clamouring and pointing. No one seems to notice you. As you edge forward to take a closer look, you see only a muddle of leaves and a pair of large, frightened eyes.

"We've caught him! We've caught the monster!" shouts out a man wearing forest clothes.

"Ugh! He's so ugly!" exclaims another.

Now other villagers chime in.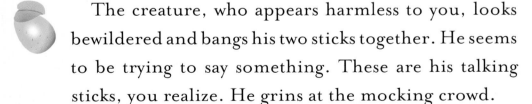

"Phooey. He smells like a pond!"

"His skin's all prickly and bristly!"

"What shall we do with him?"

The creature, who appears harmless to you, looks bewildered and bangs his two sticks together. He seems to be trying to say something. These are his talking sticks, you realize. He grins at the mocking crowd.

"Stupid monster! Stupid sticks!" shouts a small boy, throwing a rotten mango at the monster.

The monster picks it up, sniffs it and turns it over. Then he puts it carefully to one side to keep it safe.

"He doesn't even know it's rotten," says a girl.

You watch the villagers throw more fruit at him — black bananas and bruised pineapples. Thinking they are gifts, the confused monster tries to catch them.

Then someone throws a coconut at him. Others throw stones. These are hard and they really hurt. One of the stones hits the poor monster in the eye. He blinks, shudders and picks it up from the ground. He rubs it against his chest, then tries to bite it.

Now a little girl starts to laugh. What a funny, silly monster. The child moves away from her mother to take a closer look. Then, all of a sudden, she slips. You're horrified when, the next moment, she's down in the pit with the huge, hairy, green monster!

A great cry goes up from the crowd.

"The monster's got my child!" shouts the mother.

"He'll tear her to pieces!"

"He'll eat her alive! What shall we do?"

The monster reaches out to the child, who doesn't seem the least bit frightened.

He looks at her curiously. Then, very carefully, he picks her up and cradles her in his arms. With his big, hairy, green hands, he strokes her head tenderly.

The people in the crowd, who cannot see how gentle the monster is being, shout, "Give her back!"

Straightaway, the monster tries to pass the child into the villagers' grasping arms. But he can't reach.

"A rope! Someone get a rope. And a basket!" calls out the child's mother, frantic with worry.

Quickly, two villagers lower a basket on the end of a rope into the pit. You wonder what the monster will do. Will he escape and leave the little girl alone?

But, no! To the villagers' surprise, he gently places the child in the basket, where she's soon hauled to safety.

You wait to see what the child does. Does she reach out for her mother? No! She puts out her arms to the monster, who is still in the deep, dark pit.

The monster taps his sticks together again. This time you can hear a tune. The crowd hears the tune, too, and a soft murmuring begins.

62

"Listen, he's making music now. He may be a monster, but he's clever and he has a good heart."

"He saved my little girl from harm and gave her back to me," says the child's mother.

"Haul him up," shouts someone else.

And that's what they do. The monster is accepted by the welcoming crowd and they see how gentle he really is. They shower him with gifts of fresh fruit. You watch as they stroke him and hug him. How happy you feel for this lovable creature. He might *look* like a monster, but he's kind and sensitive and thoughtful, just like you!

Affirmations

- Sometimes, if other people appear different, it's easy to get the wrong idea about them. Try not to judge people before you know or understand them.
- It's easy to feel safe in a group and to gang up on someone who's unlike you. Instead, try to be thoughtful and kind to others, especially if they might be feeling scared and alone.
- Throughout life you'll meet all sorts of people who will be quite different from you. Even if they appear strange or live differently from you, be kind and try to make friends with them.

The Red Trumpet Flowers

Close your eyes and listen — listen carefully to everything around you. Can you hear that sound? It's not very loud, nor is it sharp, nor shrill. It isn't a croak, a squawk or a squeak, a grunt or a growl, a whoop or a whistle. "Hummmm, hummmm, it goes, softly. "Hummmm, hummmm," once again. What kind of creature makes this noise and where does it come from? Let's see if you can find out! Pick up your magic lantern and walk down the Enchanted Path. Where will it lead you tonight?

You find yourself at the bottom of a large garden, in the shade of a tall leafy tree. It's springtime and the garden is alive with the sounds of insects and squirrels scurrying around. High in the treetops, birds chirp and trill their sweet songs. But listen! There's that sound again. How curious this is, you think to yourself.

65

Just then, a movement above your head catches your eye. You look up in surprise and glimpse, just for a moment, something small shimmering in the sunlight. Then, in the blink of an eye, it disappears. Quickly, you spin around to see if you can find out where it's gone. "Hummmm, hummmm," you hear again, but this time the sound is much closer — right next to the rim of your brand new red hat.

Now you stand very still, not moving a muscle. What is this small creature gleaming beside you? Is it a bumblebee busily buzzing? Or a beautiful butterfly fluttering by? Maybe it's a dragonfly trying to dazzle you? Or perhaps it's a fairy whistling in the wind?

All of a sudden, you feel something brush very lightly across your cheek. You swivel your head around and a magical sight comes into view. There, dancing in the light, with feathers all the colours of the rainbow, is the tiniest, shiniest bird you've ever seen. Up and down she swoops; backward and forward, she darts; sideways she zips. Then she stops in mid-air, beating her silvery wings so fast that you can barely see them at all. "Hummmm,

hummmm," you hear. With every beat, "hummmm, hummmm."

Then, to your amazement, the tiny, shiny, little bird flies straight into you, and jabs her long, thin beak into your brand new red hat. How curious this is, you think to yourself.

"Hey, why did you do that?" you shout.

Quick as a flash, the bird darts backward, cocks her head and gazes at you with a quizzical look. "Well, ruffle my feathers!" she trills, "I thought you were a flower, the kind that gives me sweet nectar." And off she flies to the far corner of the garden, where a clump of red flowers sways gently in the breeze.

You run after the bird, then stop just in time to see her almost disappear down one of the flowers, one that looks like a little red trumpet. Then out she pops. She hovers like a tiny whirling helicopter and pokes her long bill down another red flower.

Now the bird flies over to you and spills a drop of nectar on to your finger. "Go on, taste it," she chirps. So you do just that. How sweet it is, how sticky it is! Just like runny honey, you think.

"Is this what you eat?" you ask the bird.

"I've collected it for my chicks. It'll make them grow big and strong just like me," she replies, very proudly. And off she darts once again. Up, up she flies, through the leaves of a tree dappled by sunlight to feed her two nestlings the food she has gathered.

But, oh dear! What's happening to the red trumpet flowers? In horror, you watch as a woman cuts one from its stalk with her sharp scissors.

"Stop, stop!" you call out. "Please leave those red trumpet flowers to grow tall and strong."

Puzzled, the woman stops what she's doing and looks into your eyes. "What's this all about?" she says rather sternly. "I've come to pick flowers."

You explain how important the flowers are to your new little friend. How she uses them to feed her two babies. How beautiful red trumpet flowers, like these, have lots of sweet nectar.

Just then, the tiny, shiny bird swoops into view. "Hummmm, hummmm," go her wings, and she dives down the biggest trumpet flower of all.

"Of course, silly me, I'd forgotten," says the woman. "Little hummingbirds, like this one, love these red flowers. You're right, I should leave them to grow tall and strong." And off she wanders to the other side of the garden.

"Thank you," trills the little bird. Then she flies back to her chicks with another load of sweet nectar.

In wonder, you watch her, the tiniest, shiniest bird you've ever seen in your life, dancing, spinning and twirling through the air. And now you know what kind of bird she is too. "Hummmm, hummmm," go the hummingbird's silvery wings, catching the sunlight. With every beat, "hummmm, hummmm."

Affirmations

- Listen carefully, very carefully, and you'll hear sounds you might never have heard before.
- Look for and be aware of the creatures and plants that live around you. Then you can marvel at all the things they can do.
- Being willing to learn new things will help you to find joy and excitement throughout your life.
- Understanding how animals, birds and plants live teaches you about nature. It also teaches you how to look after them and help them if you can.

The Rainbow Cat

Close your eyes and think about all the different kinds of days there are. Why are some days so dull and others so interesting? Why do some seem long and others short? Why can't every day be bright? Maybe we can banish boring days. Let's see if we can find out! Pick up your magic lantern and walk down the Enchanted Path. Where will it lead you tonight?

You find yourself in the middle of one of those dull, boring days. You gaze around you and everything appears grey and gloomy. But then you hold up your magic lantern. It glows brightly and, as you look closely, you realize it's full of lively colours – magical, multi-coloured lights. And look, there's a movement, soft as a shadow! You see the flick of a tail, the curl of a body and bright, bouncing whiskers. It's the Rainbow Cat, the cat that lights up empty, boring days.

The cat yawns, blinks, then licks his paws. Now he rubs against your ankles. He weaves in and out of the coloured lights. He skips away a little with his tail curled up like a big, furry question mark.

You follow the happy cat down a long, winding path. It leads you to a shimmering silver bridge that stretches across a deep valley. It looks so fragile, as if suspended by spiders' webs. The cat has seen a butterfly and begins to chase it over the bridge. He looks back at you. "Come on," he seems to say. "Come and play with me."

You're a little afraid as you don't know where the bridge will lead you. But the Rainbow Cat is so full of life and movement, and the butterfly is fluttering so merrily around him, that you soon forget your fears.

You step on to the bridge. You have to walk very carefully — slowly, slowly, step by shining step. Now you stop to look behind you. The silver bridge has completely disappeared! You look in front of you. There's nothing there! Only in the circle of light shed by the lantern can you see the bridge at all. It holds you, safe as a cradle, in the present moment. And it's a lovely place to be, with the Rainbow Cat skipping around you, so perfectly happy and at ease. You feel more confident now and step into the next moment, and the next — each step lighting up your day.

Is it your lantern, or is it the cat, lighting up the bridge as you go? Or maybe it's you — because if you always try to trust and enjoy each moment, your day will seem much more exciting. And if you look on the bright side, even on a dull day, you'll discover all sorts of wonderful, magical things. Now you can make every day a fun day, and banish boring days for ever!

Affirmations

- Enjoy each moment as it happens, rather than thinking or worrying about what will happen next. Each moment has something special of its own to offer you.
- Not every moment is bright and interesting, but in your mind you can always lighten things up.
- Trust that, although not every moment will be the same, every one is as precious and unique as the next.
- Feel positive about each moment as it happens and you will be positive always. This will help you with everything you do.

Granny Dean's
New Home

Close your eyes and think of a favourite place, somewhere you enjoy being most, somewhere you feel safe and loved. What would it be like if you had to leave that place or you couldn't go there anymore? Let's see if you can find out! Pick up your magic lantern and walk down the Enchanted Path. Where will it lead you tonight?

You're at Granny Dean's house. She's the granny of your best friend, Sam, and she's lived in this house, beside the sea, for as long as you can remember. It's a big, old house and even though the wind rattles the windows, it always seems cosy and welcoming. The house is filled with pictures that Granny Dean has painted and things that she's collected from the seashore. She used to travel up and down the coast when Grandpa Dean was alive, but now that she's on her own, she spends more time at home, alone.

Whenever you and Sam come to stay, Granny Dean lets you sleep in the big room in the attic, right at the top of the house. You always feel a sense of excitement as you climb up the creaky wooden stairs. How much you like it here, in this room with its slanting roof, where you can listen to the waves crashing against the sandy beach, far below the cliff on which the old house stands. How much you like it here where, out of the big oval window, you can watch the seagulls soaring over the clear blue waters, dipping and tipping their wings into the frothy surf. They're the seagulls that wake you each morning, squawking and screeching as they follow the fishing boats out to sea.

There's always something to do at Granny Dean's. You remember the time when she took you and Sam to Cowrie Cove, where you sat on the rocks dangling your feet in the water. Suddenly, the stillness of the ocean was broken by a dolphin leaping out and crashing back in again. You watched with delight as he rolled around in the sea. Then, as quickly as he'd appeared, he slid back beneath the water and swam silently away. How excited you were then.

Today, you're hoping that Granny Dean will take you and Sam to Barnacle Bay to hunt for crabs in the rock pools. You decide to go and ask her, but as you reach the bottom of the stairs, you hear her talking softly to Sam. Quietly, you open the door and Granny Dean beckons you to sit down.

"Today, I'm going to take you somewhere you've never been before," she says. "It's the place I'm going to move to when I sell this big old house."

"Oh, no, Granny!" gasps Sam. "You can't possibly leave this great house. It's the best place ever."

"It's taken me a long time to make this difficult decision," replies Granny Dean, gently taking hold of Sam's hand. "But I know I must go. The house is too big for me on my own, and I get lonely by myself without Grandpa Dean."

"But you've got us!" exclaims Sam, pointing at you and himself. "And Mum and Dad. This is *our* home too!"

Just then, a tear rolls down Granny Dean's cheek, and you know that she's as upset as Sam about moving. So you run over and give her a hug.

"My granny was sad when she moved, too," you tell her. "But she's happy now that she's settled into her new home. And she has lots of new friends."

Granny Dean smiles. "Come on, you two," she says. "Let's go and see our new house. It's not far away."

In the crystal morning sunshine, Granny Dean drives down a long sandy track and over a little bridge to the other side of the bay. Before long, you stop outside a pretty wooden house with a red roof and painted green shutters, not far from the beach. Other similar houses stand nearby.

When you get out of the car, a jolly man, about the same age as Granny Dean, comes to greet you.

"Welcome to 'The Dunes', Mrs Dean," he says cheerfully. "We're so looking forward to you living next door."

As soon as you walk through the door of Granny Dean's new house, you know she'll be happy here. It has such a good feeling about it, and it's full of sunlight. Although it's much smaller than the old house on the cliff, there are two bedrooms, so you and Sam can still come to stay.

Out of the bedroom window, you can still see the ocean and hear all the loud seagulls squawking and screeching. You can smell the salty water and the seaweed that's been washed up on the sand. And how pleased you are to discover that the beach is much closer to this house than it was to the old house on the cliff.

Just then, you notice there's a strong breeze coming off the water, which makes the windows rattle, just a little. Perhaps Granny Dean's new home won't be so different after all. You might like it even more than her old house. It's quite possible, isn't it?

Affirmations

- There's no need to be afraid of change. Doing something new can often lead to a better and happier life.
- It's not always easy to make big decisions, but if you know that it's best to change something, don't put off deciding to do it. Be brave and do what you think is right.
- Help and encourage the people you love when they make decisions, even if you suspect the result might not be to your liking.
- Sometimes people get lonely when they're on their own. Having other people around often makes them feel glad.

An Elf's Tale

Close your eyes and imagine you're on a rocky path walking up a steep mountain. On one side of the path is a deep ravine. Huge ferns cling to the edges like furry green threads in a big spider web. Above you, the mountain top is almost hidden in a mist of swirling cloud, but you can just glimpse a stone castle standing proudly on the peak. Who could live in this mysterious place? Let's see if you can find out! Pick up your magic lantern and walk down the Enchanted Path. Where will it lead you tonight?

Just then, you hear someone whistling. It's a bright, cheery sound, like a bird singing on a sunny morning. There's another sound, too — tap, tap, tap.

To your amazement, a little elf carrying a basket full of fruit appears around the corner. You notice that he's walking with the

81

help of a stick, which he taps on the rocks in front of him as he makes his way slowly up the mountain.

You've never met an elf before.

"Oh, excuse me, did I startle you?" asks the elf, looking at your astonished face.

"I'm sorry. I didn't mean to stare," you mumble. "Let me carry your basket to make up for it."

"All the way to the giant's castle?" asks the elf, with a twinkle in his bright, brown eyes.

Ah, so that's who lives in the big stone castle at the top of the mountain, you guess, starting to worry a little. You've always been rather afraid of giants. Somehow the elf has guessed this and decides to reassure you.

"Sit down for a moment," he says, gently. "And let me tell you the most amazing story."

"Is it a frightening story?" you ask quickly.

The elf shakes his head. "No, it's about how I came to walk with a cane, and why I am taking this basket of fruit to a giant who lives on top of a mountain."

The elf taps his wooden cane on a rock, like a drumstick playing a tune on a drum.

"Before I used this walking stick," he begins, "I loved to leap from rock to rock along this path."

Pointing to the vines hanging across the ravine, he adds, "I used to swing on those vines and scramble up and over the edge like a squirrel."

"What happened next?" you ask curiously.

"Then one day I was sitting high up in a tree when a giant ran past underneath. The ground was slippery and suddenly he stumbled. He grabbed the tree to stop himself from falling into the ravine. And that's when the tree bent over and I tumbled out on to the ground, which was very hard."

"What a terrible thing to happen!" you gasp.

"Yes, but I was lucky," says the elf. "I could have broken my neck — instead I only broke a leg."

"Surely the giant didn't leave you on this lonely mountainside all by yourself?" you shriek.

"You forget how enormous giants are," replies the elf. "He had no idea that I was in the tree, so he didn't know what harm he'd done."

"Then, then how …?" you blurt out.

"Wait and listen," says the elf. "That night it began to snow. I knew my only chance of being rescued was if someone heard me. So I propped myself against the tree and began to whistle like a blackbird."

"And the giant heard you?" you ask amazed.

"Giants have enormous ears and very sharp hearing," explains the elf. "And everyone knows that blackbirds don't sing at night." Then he pauses and adds slowly and quietly, "The giant saved my life."

"But it was his fault in the first place!" you exclaim. "I'd have been really angry with him."

"What would be the point?" replies the elf. "It was an accident. Forgive and forget, that's my motto."

The elf reaches for the basket, but you take it quickly. It's much heavier than you thought and you wonder how on earth the little elf could have carried it so far.

"I still don't understand," you say, looking rather puzzled. "Why are you taking fruit to the giant?"

"Because he needs my help to get better," replies the elf, shrugging his shoulders.

"But what's wrong with him?" you ask.

"He stumbled again," says the elf. "This time he was very thoughtful. He didn't grab on to a tree in case he harmed some-body else. So he ended up falling into the ravine and banging his poor head."

Now you understand that the elf is taking fruit to the giant because he hurt himself rather than risk hurting anyone else. The elf was right to forgive and forget.

As the basket grows heavier on your arm, you feel happy that you've been able to help such a kind, wise creature as the little elf. You follow your friend up the path toward the top of the mountain, as he taps his walking stick on the rocks ahead and whistles merrily. By the time the stone castle comes into view, you discover that you're no longer afraid of giants. Like elves, they can be kind and thoughtful as well. So you start to whistle, too, just like a blackbird.

Affirmations

- When something unfortunate happens by accident or mistake, there's no point in blaming anyone or anything. It's best to be kind, patient and understanding, and help in any way you can.
- Holding on to bad or angry feelings only makes you unhappy. You'll feel much better if you forgive and forget.
- Seeing a situation from another person's point of view often helps you to understand your own fears and worries.
- It always helps to own up to your mistakes and to make up for them however you can. This will make you feel much better, too!

The
Magic Meadow

Close your eyes and imagine that you're leaping like a frog through a magic meadow. You bound around in the most carefree way, as if you've done it all your life. But, how can this be? Let's see if you can find out! Pick up your magic lantern and follow the Enchanted Path. Where will it lead you tonight?

You feel just as you normally do, except that you have amazing leapy legs. Leap! Over a hump. Leap! Over a stream. Leap! Over a bush. Have you turned into a frog? No! But wait a minute — what is this? As you look down, you see that you do indeed have leapy frog's legs. How did you come to have those?

Right now, you don't care. You just want to show off your new magic leaping skills. But suddenly you see a squirrel up a tree with a wonderful bushy, red tail. You've never noticed just how good a squirrel's tail looks before — all bright and bushy.

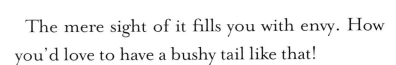

The mere sight of it fills you with envy. How you'd love to have a bushy tail like that!

In a second, the squirrel has lost his bushy tail and you have one instead. What a strange place this is! As soon as you wish for something, you seem to get it. You're very happy, but the squirrel looks most upset. Nevertheless, you leap around on your leapy legs, playing with your bushy tail. Leap, leap. Swish, swish. Who can you show off to now?

Behind a fence you see a donkey with long, whiskery ears. The same feeling comes over you again. You want ears like that. What a figure you'd make then. And guess what? Suddenly, the donkey has lost his ears. Where are they? They're on your head, of course!

You leap around, with your leapy legs, your bushy tail and your long ears. You head toward a pond to admire your reflection in the water. But, before you reach it, you hear the sad sound of sobbing.

"Someone's stolen my legs," wails a little frog.

"Someone's stolen my tail," cries the squirrel.

"Someone's stolen my ears," moans the donkey.

Now a rather swanky feeling comes over you. "Look over here," you shout out to the animals.

Then you wag your long, whiskery ears, swish your bushy tail and leap on your leapy legs.

The animals stop sobbing and start to laugh and laugh. They've never seen a creature like it! You look at your reflection in the pond. And neither have you! What could look sillier than a frog without a leap, a squirrel without a tail and a donkey without long ears? Why, somebody with all three, like you, of course! Now you don't want them anymore.

Luckily, this is a magic meadow where wishes come true, so they're soon back with their rightful owners. And, you're happy to be yourself again, with your own legs, your own ears, and no bushy, red tail in sight.

 Affirmations

- When you feel jealous or envious of other people or of what they have, remember how lucky you are to be you. There will never be another person in the world exactly like you. This makes you special and unique.
- Be happy for the things you have and the person you are, and be comfortable with how you look.
- Concentrate on what you have, rather than what you don't have.
- Be glad when your friends have something you like. Maybe they will share it with you, just as you would share it with them.

A Bed
for Winter

Close your eyes and imagine you're deep in the woods. You know it's autumn because the leaves on the trees are red and yellow and orange. And even though the sun is shining and the sky is deep blue, there's a crispness in the air. All around you animals are scurrying here and there. You can hear them so clearly and you listen to every movement they make. But why are these animals so busy? Let's see if you can find out! Pick up your magic lantern and walk down the Enchanted Path. Where will it lead you tonight?

In front of you, a mouse is burrowing under the roots of a tree looking for a warm place to curl up and sleep through the winter. But will he find somewhere safe and cosy? As he disappears into the ground, the mouse looks up at you. "Don't worry about me," he says, "I know what I'm doing."

Above you, a furry red squirrel chatters high in the branches. She's carrying an armful of acorns to store in her nest. You know she'll need lots of acorns to last her through the winter. But will she find enough? Will there be room to store them all? The squirrel looks at you with her bright eyes. "Don't worry about me," she says, "I know what I'm doing."

All of a sudden, a mother bear and her cub lumber past you. You step back, but you're not afraid. The glossy brown bears barely notice you're there — they're too busy eating. You watch them gobbling nuts, seeds and red berries. Then they scratch up the brown earth with their big, curved claws looking for insects and worms. You know that they'll need to eat as much food as they can before they find a dark cave to sleep in for the winter. But will they find enough food before the first snow falls, you wonder? And where will they find a cave that's big enough for both of them to shelter from the freezing cold? The mother bear looks at you with her large, clever eyes. "Don't worry about me," she says. "I know what I'm doing."

Just then, a tall tree crashes down behind you. You jump back, startled, and cry out loud in surprise.

"I'm sorry I frightened you," says a beaver, standing beside the fallen tree, as he gnaws off a leafy branch with his big, sharp teeth. "I'm taking this to store in my lodge, so I can eat it during the long winter."

You look around you. You can't see a lodge anywhere or indeed anything that looks like a shelter against icy winter winds. As if he's reading your mind, the beaver points to a big mound of sticks in the middle of a lake. "That's my lodge," he says, proudly. "That's where I live with my family during the cold winter."

Looking out across the lake, you see other beavers dragging long branches with their mouths through the rippling water. Suddenly they dive down, taking the big branches with them. "But you have to swim to reach your lodge," you say, shivering at the thought. "Doesn't the water make you very cold?"

"Our fur is waterproof," explains the chatty beaver. "We don't feel the cold."

"What if the water freezes over?" you ask.

"What if you run out of food?"

"You worry too much," replies the beaver. "Come with me and I'll show you my lodge. Then you won't have to worry anymore."

"But it's much too cold," you say, trembling a little. "And I don't know how to swim underwater."

The beaver looks deep into your eyes. "Trust me," he says. "Just pretend you're a beaver."

And it works! All at once, you're swimming with the beaver and you don't even feel cold! Shoals of silver fish pass by and other beavers paddle beside you carrying more branches and bark in their mouths.

Bravely, you follow the beaver through an underwater tunnel and come up into his lodge. Inside is a small round room made of sticks and mud. There's a thick carpet of dry grass on the floor, and the air is warm and smells faintly of hay. In one corner is a huge pile of branches with lots of green shoots and leaves for the beavers to eat during the winter. You lie down on the dry grass beside two little beavers. They quickly look up at you, and then they close their eyes sleepily. You're so comfortable that you feel *you* could fall fast asleep, too.

"Now you can see why there's no need to worry," says the beaver as he drags over his branch and piles it on top of some others. "We have everything we need here to last through the winter and we'll be safe and snug in our warm, cosy beds."

Now you understand that all the animals know just what they're doing. Still lying between the two sleepy beavers, you close your eyes and wonder what they are dreaming. Are they dreaming of big snowflakes falling silently through the air, of sunlight bouncing off an icy lake, or perhaps of the new green shoots that will grow for them to eat in the springtime?

Affirmations

- People often know more than you think. If you respect other people's knowledge, you'll find out all sorts of interesting things.
- When you try to guess what's in someone else's mind, always remember that it's only a guess!
- Don't worry too much about things you don't understand. They usually become clear in the end.
- Don't forget that, although sometimes you will be right, there will be other times when you may be wrong.
- Learn to trust others, just as you would want them to trust you.

Dancing with Moon Sprites

Close your eyes and think about a party invitation. Imagine you're holding it in your hand — a pure white envelope with silver lettering. Who is it from and where have you been asked to go? Let's see if you can find out! Pick up your magic lantern and walk down the Enchanted Path. Where will it lead you tonight?

You tear open the white envelope and pull out a card, edged with silver. "Come to the Crystal Party," it says. But there's no name on the invitation, and no address. Then you see the words, "To find the party, just follow the clear light in your magic lantern. Trust where it takes you and you'll find your way."

You raise your magic lantern and stand in its circle of light. Then you notice that one light, a bright white light, is clearer than all the others. It shines like the beam of a torch, lighting the way ahead.

You begin to follow it. There's a long glowing road ahead of you, with a white door at the end. "Ah," you think, "That must be where the Crystal Party is being held tonight." So you walk toward it.

Suddenly, your lantern picks out another light, a purple light, like a coloured moonbeam. Dancing in the light is a Purple Moon Sprite. "Hey!" she shouts out. "You might not know anyone at this Crystal Party. Perhaps nobody there will talk to you. Think how embarrassing and upsetting that would be."

With that, the Purple Moon Sprite dances ahead of you toward a shining purple door.

"Go on, come to the Purple Party!" says the Sprite.

You're unsure: the purple door is closer and the Sprite is so friendly. What should you do?

In the end, you decide to do as the invitation asks, so you follow the bright white light of your lantern.

A little further along there's another beam of light. This time it's yellow. And sure enough, dancing in its rays is a Yellow Moon Sprite. "Hey!" calls out the Sprite, rather cheekily. "This Crystal Party you're going to. Maybe you won't like anyone there. Maybe they won't like you."

And the jolly Yellow Sprite dances up a yellow path to a shiny yellow door. "Come to the Yellow Party instead," he beckons you.

Now you feel confused. The yellow door looks inviting, too. Which party should you go to?

But, once again, you decide not to be misled, and you follow the white light toward the gleaming silver door.

You've only gone a few steps when a Blue Moon Sprite comes dancing around your head.

"So you're going to the Crystal Party. What if it's really boring and there is absolutely nothing there to interest you. You would have to sit still and make polite conversation the whole time," she chatters. "Come with me to the Blue Party instead. There'll be great games to play."

Oh dear! What should you do? All these coloured parties sound such fun and so tempting.

Before you know it, a Red Moon Sprite is there beside you, teasing you and filling you with doubt.

"Are you sure you're dressed well enough for the Crystal Party?" she says. "Everyone will be glamorous and they might stare at you. You'll look silly and out of place."

Now you're in a real muddle. Purple, yellow, blue, red — there are coloured Moon Sprites everywhere you look. The playful Sprites are each beckoning you to go in a different direction. And you're so worried about this Crystal Party. If only someone would tell you what to do.

Your head is in a whirl, but suddenly, as you hold your lantern up higher, you somehow know exactly what you must do. It's simple. You must follow the lantern's clear white light right to the very end of the glowing path — to the shining white door. So off you set, pleased that you've stuck to your initial decision.

Before you, the door is open and the sweet sound of crystal-clear music wafts toward you. Feeling very excited, you step through the shimmering doorway.

And there to welcome you is a warm and friendly face. It's the Crystal Moon Sprite. She gives you a hug and offers you a sparkling crystal tunic to wear to her party. You slip it on. It fits perfectly. "I'm so pleased you came," she says, smiling.

Just then, you see all the coloured Moon Sprites dancing their way to the door. They've followed you and seen the great welcome you've received. The bright white light, which is so clear and pure, seems to have drawn them to the Crystal Party.

The Sprites tell you they're sorry that they tried to tempt you away from this wonderful party, and how happy they are that you didn't listen to them. Then they mingle together, filling the room with light.

And you're so glad that you did what you believed was the right thing to do. Now you've made a new friend who you've made very happy; someone you can play and laugh with — a good friend for ever.

Affirmations

- Always do what you believe is the right thing to do, even if someone else tries to change your mind. It will work out better in the end.
- If you're true to yourself, you'll find people who are loyal to you, and the things that really matter.
- When you're asked to do something, don't look around to see what others are doing. Make your own choice. It may be the best one of all.
- If others make fun of you for doing things differently, don't worry. It's important to believe in yourself. When you do this, you'll be amazed how others will believe in you, too.

The Monkey King

Close your eyes and imagine you're standing in a jungle clearing, surrounded by exotic flowers. The ground is covered in petals and their sweet perfume hangs in the air. Just then, a crowd of boys and girls, so small that they barely come up to your knees, burst in from the shadows. What are they doing here? Let's see if you can find out! Pick up your magic lantern and walk down the Enchanted Path. Where will it lead you tonight?

You kneel down so you can see the children more clearly. The girls are dressed in yellow petal skirts with garlands of tiny blue flowers on top of their heads. The boys, wearing leafy capes, have red and blue feathers poked into their hair.

"We've come from our home deep in the jungle to dance for the Monkey King," a boy tells you proudly. "He was crowned our leader this very day."

You watch the children practise their steps as they wait for the King. But one girl stands all alone. While the others are smiling, she's frowning. You wonder why. Then you see her touch the top of her head and you realize that she's lost her garland of flowers.

A boy walks over to her. "Please join in, Sun Lily," you hear him say. "Don't worry about your headdress. The Monkey King won't mind you not having one."

"But I'll look different from everyone else," says Sun Lily. "Dance without me. It won't matter anyway!"

But the other dancers look worried and you sense that it *does* matter to them. They've practised together for months. Without Sun Lily the dance won't be the same.

Now the sound of drums fills the air.

"The Monkey King's coming!" cries a boy.

You know that you must help Sun Lily before the King arrives. But how? Then you have an idea. You ask each girl to give you one flower from her garland. Then, as quickly as you can, you weave the stems together and create a garland just like the others.

"Please try it on, Sun Lily," you say very gently.

As you place the perfect new garland on her tiny head, Sun Lily turns toward you with tears of joy glistening in her eyes. "Thank you," she whispers into your ear. "I was silly to say I wouldn't dance. I just wanted to look as pretty as all the others."

At that moment, a monkey wearing a crown of big orange flowers takes his place on a wooden throne. The dancers move forward. You watch as Sun Lily leaps and twirls in front of him, a happy smile spread across her face. The Monkey King looks away from the dancing and catches your eye. He nods as if to say "thank you", and you understand that he knows what you have done.

Affirmations

- When you work as part of a team, it's important not to let anyone else down. There's almost always a way to solve a problem when you take the time to think about it.
- It's best to share your problems, rather than keep them to yourself. In this way others can help you to reach a good solution.
- Sometimes it's difficult to do something you don't want to do, but you may have to be unselfish to make other people happy.
- Remember that you don't have to be the same as everyone else — everyone is different, so just be yourself.

Bubbles of
Laughter

Close your eyes and imagine a beautiful, big, bright bubble hovering in the air above you. How fragile it seems, how delicate it looks — ready to burst at any moment. But what is it doing there, spinning, dancing and shimmering in front of you? Let's see if you can find out! Pick up your magic lantern and walk down the Enchanted Path. Where will it lead you tonight?

You follow the bubble as it bobs ahead of you. And soon there are lots more perfect, transparent, round bubbles floating beside you, all making strange gurgling noises. They sound almost as if they're laughing!

As you watch them, you suddenly feel yourself lifted up, up and away — on a soft carpet of bubbles. You don't know where the bubbles are taking you, but the further you travel, the duller and darker it becomes.

After a while, the bubble carpet stops, and you step off into a rather dreary street, in the middle of a grey-looking town.

Why are you here, you wonder? It's as if the bubbles have brought you here for a reason. There are people going about their business, but none of them seem to be very happy. Even the children on their way to school are walking wearily and speaking to each other in quiet, hushed voices.

A few of the bubbles detach themselves and drift close to the children, but just out of their reach. A small girl spots them and starts to leap in the air trying to catch them. Then, more and more bubbles — glimmering silver ones, gleaming pink ones, glistening purple ones — make a shining circle around the school children, who start to laugh and clap their hands. Soon all the children are laughing and chasing the bubbles that keep on appearing.

Mothers holding babies come out of their houses. What's all this noise they can hear in the streets? In delight, the babies start gurgling happily and waving their chubby fingers as the bubbles dance around them.

Now the bubbles are floating higher and higher. Men and women in office buildings, who've heard the commotion, throw open their windows to watch the bubbles float past — spinning and wheeling, swooping and twisting. How happy they are to see their children having such a good time. Forgetting their work for a while, they start smiling, joking and laughing together.

Through the winding streets, the dancing, giggling children follow the gurgling bubbles. Shopkeepers leave their stores empty to watch the fun, pointing and laughing as the children rush by. Past the town hall and the police station, the post office and the fire station, the bubbles continue their long journey, as they head for the old people's home and then on to the hospital. It's clear to you that they want everyone in this town to be happy today.

When the old people hear the loud laughter ringing down the street, they look up from their televisions and rise from their chairs. They forget their stiff joints and make for the windows, reminding one another of how much they used to love blowing and chasing bubbles when they were children. Long after the bubbles and children have passed by, the old people stand around beaming, as they talk to each other about their childhood memories.

Next, the procession makes its way to the town hospital. Some of the bubbles stay outside and dance with the children, while others bob up and down the long hospital corridors. You slip in among them, surrounded by the sound of people laughing. You peep through the windows at the patients and watch in amazement as they sit up and grin when the joyful people and bubbles go by. It's as if the happy noise of laughter is helping them to feel better.

All this amusement has made the children very late for school. So, like a shoal of shimmering fish, the bubbles turn around and lead them back to where their schoolbags are sitting. How different the street seems to be now. It's not dull, dreary and dark any more: the sun is shining, the birds are singing, the dogs are barking and people all around are chatting and smiling. Laughter seems to have brought the whole place alive.

When the children go into school, the bubbles lift you up again to take you home. Everyone waves good-bye — not only to you, but also to the perfect, beautiful bubbles that have brought them such pleasure.

Before long, you're back at home, safe and sound. Dancing your way back to bed, you realize that the bubbles wanted to show you just how important it is to be happy and to laugh lots. As you drift off to sleep, you think about things that always make you laugh and feel happy: silly jokes, birthday cake, and, of course, clowns; and now, you can include bubbles, too! Who'd ever have thought that bubbles could be so much fun?

Affirmations

- Laughter makes people feel good. Try to laugh every day.
- Having a good sense of humour and being able to laugh makes life fun and interesting, and helps when things become difficult.
- Laughter is infectious. Share your laughter with others. When you laugh, it can make other people laugh, too.
- You can find laughter and happiness in almost every situation — it's just a matter of looking for it.
- There's a saying that goes: "Laughter is the best medicine". It's true. Laughter really can help people to get well.

The
Mud Man

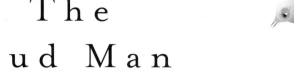

Close your eyes and imagine a wonderful garden, where elegant plants grow along paths that wind through blossoming trees and neatly clipped hedges. Gardeners work from morning to night tending the beautiful flowers that are on show for everyone to see. But there's something even more special about this garden. What can it be? Let's see if you can find out! Pick up your magic lantern and walk down the Enchanted Path. Where will it lead you tonight?

You open a door in a wall that must be a secret entrance to another part of the garden. Inside, it's cool and still. Sweet scents waft to you on the gentlest of breezes, as you watch people wander from flower bed to flower bed, admiring what they see.

The bees buzz as they go about their work, and the birds are singing. But you can hear other tinkly little voices, too. How strange! It's the flowers that are talking!

Can anyone else hear them speaking, you wonder? You listen carefully to pick out what the flowers are saying.

"Of course, the adults come especially to see us," say the delphiniums. "They come to admire and wonder at our rare blue colour, so they can compare us to the sky high above."

"Nonsense!" reply the hollyhocks, tall as church spires. "You're all the same colour. People come to marvel at all our reds, pinks, purples and yellows."

You gaze at the delphiniums and the hollyhocks. To you, they're all equally beautiful. The flowers, who seem unaware that you're there, continue to talk between themselves, and you pretend not to listen.

"Children, on the other hand, usually want to visit the Mud Man in the trees," says the tallest hollyhock of all. " I can't think why. He's ugly and stupid, stuck in the mud all the time!" All the flowers laugh rudely.

You're wondering about the Mud Man when you hear a little boy saying to his mother, "I'm bored with flowers. It says here that visitors might like to see the man in the woods who's made from mud and grass. Can we go and look for him now?"

Ah, so that's what the flowers are talking about, you think to yourself. So, you decide to follow the little boy and his mother as they disappear into the woods.

On the way, you hear more flowers bragging and boasting to each other. "We're the tallest," they say, or, "We smell the sweetest," and, "Look at us — we're the most beautiful flowers in the world."

You leave the main gardens behind and follow the little boy and his mother along one of the twisting paths. It's dark and cool in the woods.

Just then, the little boy runs off, playing hide-and-go-seek with his mother. You're so busy watching them, that at first you don't realize what's straight in front of you, returning your stare. But there it is: a massive man's head made from mud, moss and grass, rising from the earth. You can see his grassy hair, his big muddy nose and his huge mouth, but the rest of his body seems to be under the ground.

As you stand all alone beside the Mud Man, you wonder — Is he real? Does he speak too?

"Hello," he says, cheerily, showing his big, white, stony teeth in a wide, friendly smile.

"Have you seen lots of beautiful flowers today?"

"I have," you answer, wondering how the flowers could possibly have thought this man made of mud was stupid. To you, he speaks like a gentleman.

The Mud Man seems to read your mind. "Don't worry what the flowers say about me," he adds. "I don't. They're all perfectly lovely in their own way. I adore them, even though they like to laugh at me. But every year they bloom, droop and then fade away. I never leave — I'm here all the time in this wonderful garden, so I see them come and I see them go."

"Do you mind being stuck here?" you ask, wondering how far down into the earth his body must go, considering the enormous size of his head.

"Oh, I'm not really stuck at all," he replies. "The flowers think I'm rooted to one spot, just like they are. But, at night, I sometimes get up and wander around this beautiful garden."

" What if someone sees you?" you ask the Mud Man curiously.

"Ah, I don't do it in the daytime, or I'd frighten the visitors!" he says. "Anyway, I'm really quite happy here.

The earth keeps my body warm. Mud might not be pretty, but it's glorious stuff. And I might not be pretty either, but I'm quite happy and the children love me and always come back to see me."

At that moment, you hear the mother call her son to come and look. The Mud Man gives you a wink, stops talking and stays still as a statue, and you understand that he only talks to children. It's time for you to go.

As you follow the winding path out of the garden, you feel lucky to have met the Mud Man. Even though he wasn't as elegant as the proud talking flowers, you'll always remember how friendly he was, and how happy and contented he was just to be himself.

Affirmations

- There's no need to boast or brag to get other people's attention. Good people will like you for who and what you are.
- Try not to judge other people on what they look like. On the inside, they have feelings that are similar to yours.
- If you're happy with yourself and with the way you look, there's no need to worry what other people think or say about you.
- Learning how other people live and think makes you understand them more easily, and helps you to enjoy their company.
- Always look for, enjoy and respect the good things in people.

Something to Smile About

Close your eyes and imagine a rock pool at the edge of a sandy beach. Think about the different creatures that live in this strange, wonderful, watery world. What might they be doing? Let's see if you can find out! Pick up your magic lantern and walk down the Enchanted Path. Where will it lead you tonight?

You lie down on a flat rock and look closely into a pool of clear blue water. Below you, some sea anemones, which look like small exotic flowers, cling to the rocks, waving their tentacles backward and forward. Silvery fish frolic in a forest of frondy seaweed. Nearby, a lobster with big front claws lurks lazily on a patch of soft yellow sand, watching a spiny, black sea urchin moving slowly by.

Just then, you hear a spluttery voice beside you. You turn your head and see a small red crab that seems to be speaking to you.

At first, you think the crab might nip you, but soon you realize she just wants to have a chat.

"It's not fair," she says sadly. "I wanted to go with the children. Then I could have had a ride in a bucket and maybe have shared their picnic."

The crab shuffles closer to you. "You see, two of my friends were fished out in a net this morning," she continues. "I bet they're having a wonderful time."

You're not so sure that her friends are having such a good time. The children might have forgotten all about them by now, leaving them feeling lost and lonely. But you don't want to worry your new little friend, so you focus on all the good reasons why she's so fortunate still to be here in the rock pool.

"It's so nice here," you say reassuringly. "The water's cool and there are lots of exciting places to discover."

"Maybe," the crab says doubtfully. "But that doesn't stop me from being disappointed that I'm not on an adventure like my two friends."

"Look how lucky you are to be a crab," you say. "Happy in the sea, happy on the land; able to explore the sand and rocks whenever you like. None of the other sea creatures can do that."

"You're right, I suppose. And none of the other sea creatures seem disappointed that the children didn't choose them for their bucket," replies the crab. "I wouldn't have met you if I'd been taken away, either."

Just then, a wave crashes over the rocks and you realize that it's time to leave before the pool becomes part of the sea again. You say goodbye to the friendly crab. Scuttling sideways, she waves you farewell with a grateful look in her eyes. As you run across the beach, you feel happy that you've managed to help her to understand just how good her life is, and how lucky she is to be a crab.

Affirmations

- Even when you're feeling bad about a particular situation, there are still lots of reasons to smile and be happy.
- Always make the best of everything. Even when you're disappointed, good things may come along soon.
- Be happy and contented with who you are and what you have. Remember that what others have is not necessarily better.
- There's a saying that goes: "A problem shared is a problem halved." It's true. You can often solve a problem by talking about it with other people. They will help you to feel better in any way they can.

Oodles
of Oobles

Close your eyes and imagine a land where fruits called oobles and merberries grow on trees that are purple and yellow and red. Who might live in such a place and what other strange and wonderful food might they eat? Let's see if you can find out! Pick up your magic lantern and walk down the Enchanted Path. Where will it lead you tonight?

You find yourself strolling down a path that's lined with thousands of tiny lanterns twinkling in the light of the moon. You follow the path through an orchard of purple trees laden with fruits that seem to glow in the dark. You pick a pink fruit hanging just within your reach and pop it into your mouth. It's the most delicious fruit you've ever eaten, so you pick a few more as you amble along. All around, you can see figures filling baskets with fruit plucked from the trees, but you can't really make them out in the shadows.

There seems to be something different about them. In fact, they're not like anyone you've ever seen before. Like the fruits hanging from the purple trees, they, too, seem to glow.

At the edge of the orchard, you see the lights of a crowded restaurant with a sign saying "Fragoo's Place". Gathered around the tables sit families of gleaming green people. You're about to go in and sit down, but as you draw near, someone runs up, takes your hand and pulls you toward the back door.

"Can you help me serve some pies? We're so short-staffed tonight," gasps a small green person with big eyes and pointy ears. "By the way, I'm called Mimboo — pleased to meet you."

"But where am I and who are all these glowing, green people?" you ask Mimboo, puzzled.

"We're the Tassoos and this is Ooble Land," replies Mimboo. "We make the best ooble and merberry pies in the whole wide world. They're so scrumptious and yummy that they make us glow with sheer delight whenever we eat them!"

124

You follow Mimboo inside. Under the bright yellow lights of the kitchen, you see other green people hard at work. Fragoo, the owner, is wearing a chef's hat, which makes him stand out from the others.

Before long, you're dashing in and out of the hot kitchen fetching platefuls of ooble and merberry pie, which look a bit like fruit tarts to you, except that they're in luminous colours with all kinds of exotic toppings. One of the Tassoos orders a Nooble Ooble. It's light blue, topped with a thick goo that looks like glowing honey. Another wants a Merberry Delight made with purple fruit and a frothy yellow topping.

You have to listen very carefully when you take the orders. It would be easy to mix them up and you're sure that Fragoo wouldn't be pleased if you did. Although you're working very hard, you're enjoying yourself because everyone's so friendly and everything runs like clockwork under Fragoo's stern gaze.

"You can take a break now," calls out Fragoo, just as you're starting to get tired. So you sit down outside and drink a glass of crystal clear water that sparkles, bubbles and fizzes.

At that moment, you hear someone sniffing. You look around and there, crouched down beside the kitchen wall and rubbing his eyes with his small fists, is Padoo — a tiny green person, who looks very sad.

"What's the matter?" you ask him.

"I messed up," he says sorrowfully. "I didn't listen properly to the order and I put merberries on to a Nooble Ooble by mistake. Fragoo told me off and now I'm frightened to go back into the kitchen."

"But you can't stay here on such a busy night," you say. "Fragoo needs you. Let's go back together."

Inside the kitchen, Padoo is surprised because Fragoo isn't looking angry any more.

"You made a mistake when you didn't listen, Padoo," he says, "but everyone makes mistakes. I'm sure you won't make that one again, will you? "

"No, I won't," says Padoo. "I'm sorry."

Now Fragoo is smiling. "In fact, the customer loved what you gave her, Padoo," he says. "You've just invented the Ooble Merberry Special! So dry your eyes and head out to take some more orders."

The restaurant is quieter now. You're not really needed any more, so you take off your apron and are about to leave, when Mimboo spots you.

"Thank you for your help tonight," she says. "Here, take some pie to eat on your way home." And she gives you a slice of Padoo's Ooble Merberry Special.

Mmmm, yummy, you think, glowing with delight — this is the most delicious pie in the whole wide world. Back in your bed, you dream of new ooble and merberry dishes to create, just in case you ever visit "Fragoo's Place" in Ooble Land again. Who knows, perhaps it will be "Padoo's Place" by then!

Affirmations

- While it's best to try to do things right, everybody makes mistakes sometimes, so try not to be too hard on yourself.
- If you accept that you've made a mistake and say you're sorry, people will understand and let you try again.
- It's best not to give up when you make a mistake. Sometimes they turn out to be good things and lead to something new.
- You can learn and grow from any mistake, so don't be afraid to make one. In fact, one of the worst mistakes you can make is to worry about making one!

A Curious Kangaroo

Close your eyes and imagine yourself in a hot, hot place with clear blue skies above you and red dust swirling around your feet. It's so hot that the heat of the scorching sun has baked the earth dry. Where are you, you wonder, and who might live in a place like this? Let's see if you can find out! Pick up your magic lantern and walk down the Enchanted Path. Where will it lead you tonight?

You find yourself sheltering from the sun in the shade of an acacia tree. Ahead of you, the rugged land is scattered with stumpy bushes and big, red rocks. Giant termite mounds rise from the ground like small cathedrals. A feeling of stillness is all around. You must be in the Australian outback!

Suddenly, the silence is broken by a strange sound that you've never heard before. Thump, thump, thump, it goes. Then, thump once again.

You move toward the thumping noise, and there, all alone, you see a young kangaroo beating his long, back feet on the dry, dusty ground. All at once, the little kangaroo turns to face you.

"S-s-sorry, I didn't mean to startle you," you stutter, feeling a little scared of this rather peculiar animal covered in woolly brown fur.

"No worries, I'm really pleased to see you," replies the kangaroo. "I don't like being all by myself out here in the bush. My name's Joey, who are you?"

You tell Joey your name and ask him why he's thumping his hind feet.

"I'm lost," admits Joey. "And I thought my mother might hear me if I thumped really loudly." Joey explains that he should be snuggled up safely in his mother's pouch. But he got bored and impatient and wanted to find his brother, Boomer, who's practising for the Great Kangaroo Jumping Competition. Joey strayed too far from his mob and now he's lost.

You listen to Joey's story and then ask him if any of his friends among the other creatures in the outback might be able to help him to find his mother.

"That's a bonzer idea," booms Joey excitedly. And off he bounds toward a tall eucalyptus tree next to a big red rock.

"Hey, Herbie!" he shouts out. "I'm lost. Can you spot my mother from up there?"

You look up to see who Joey is speaking to. And there, resting high on a branch, munching lazily on a bunch of shiny green leaves, is a small, grey creature with big fluffy ears that looks like a bear. It's a Koala.

"G'day, Joey," says Herbie sleepily, "Hold on a mo, I'll climb up and have a look-see."

Using his long, sharp claws, Herbie makes his way to the top of the tree. As he searches the bush, he scrunches up his leathery nose to sniff the warm air.

"Yep, I think those are kangaroos under the trees over there. Certainly smells like your mob, Joey!" annouces Herbie, pointing toward a clump of tall gum trees in the far distance. "I'll take you there. You're too young to be alone in the outback."

Herbie climbs backward down to the foot of the tall tree. After introducing himself to you, he sets off into the bush, with you and Joey close behind.

131

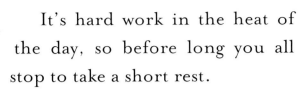

It's hard work in the heat of the day, so before long you all stop to take a short rest.

While Herbie climbs up a tree to check your position, you catch sight of an animal that looks like a wild dog with a big, bushy tail.

"G'day, Cobber," calls down Herbie to the dog, which you understand is a dingo. "We're taking this nipper back to his mother. He went walkabout last night and lost his way in the dark."

"I'll join in the search," replies Cobber gallantly, pricking up his ears. "I'll keep you all safe on the way. No one messes with a dingo, you know!"

So, together with Joey, Herbie and Cobber, the dingo, you continue your journey toward the clump of tall gum trees. Over the baked red earth you run. Under the acacia trees you go. Through the stumpy bushes you dash. Past the big termite mounds you race. And around the big, red rocks you jog. Until finally you reach the clump of tall gum trees.

As you draw near, a big kangaroo hops up to meet you — "Where've you been, Joey?" scolds his mother. "I thought I'd lost you for ever!"

Then she gives him a big long hug and thanks you, Herbie and Cobber for bringing him home safely.

To your amazement, Joey jumps headfirst into his mother's pouch and turns a complete somersault until just his head's sticking out. In an instant, he's snuggled up and fast asleep.

As the sun dips behind the horizon and the blue sky turns yellow, orange and red, Joey dreams of being a champion jumper, like his big brother Boomer, and winning the Great Kangaroo Jumping Competition … one day, when he's older and wiser … when he's good and ready. Perhaps you'll be there to cheer him on! There's always a chance, isn't there?

Affirmations

- Stay close to the people you love and trust. They are there to take care of you and to make sure you're safe.
- Try not to be in a rush to do things that you're not quite ready to do. There will be plenty of time in which to do them — as well as lots more things — in the future.
- Enjoy the things that you do well, rather than wanting to do the same things as others.
- Being part of a team makes it easier to achieve what you want, because you're working with others toward the same thing.

The Power of Visualization

The art of creating a picture in your mind – visualization – is a particularly effective method of getting children to use their imagination and of giving them power over their thinking. It's an effective tool that will be of enormous value throughout their lives, as it helps them to think beyond their boundaries, put themselves in new and unexpected situations, and project their thoughts and ideas. Visualization can also boost self-esteem, bring calm and encourage resourcefulness and creativity.

There are some short visualization exercises on pp.135–9, for you to practise with your child. Or, you could play your own visualization games together. To start with, simply ask your child to close her eyes and picture something familiar, such as a beloved toy. Get her to describe it in as much detail as possible. When she's older, she can try visualizing ideas that need a greater leap in imagination, such as a visit to the beach or a walk in the park.

Psychologists now help athletes to prepare for competitions by teaching them to imagine themselves winning. By teaching your child to visualize when she's young, you equip her with the means to enhance her personal performance as she grows up. If your child can visualize herself being calm and confident before taking an exam, it will usually have a positive effect on her result.

134

Helping Your Child
to Visualize

Teaching your child to visualize is a wonderful way to help him bring the stories in this book alive in his mind. It will also make reading them together much more meaningful, enjoyable and rewarding, as he learns to imagine himself as an integral part of each story. But it will take practice before your child will be able to consciously visualize anything that comes into his head or conjure up any image at will. At first, he may find it quite difficult to relax himself sufficiently and to concentrate enough to empty his mind and imagine a particular person, object or scene in his mind's eye. This step-by-step guide is a really good way to introduce him to the art of visualization.

Step 1

Start by encouraging your child to relax. Ask him to sit in
a relaxed but upright position with his eyes gently closed.
Then, ask him to take a few long, deep breaths.

Step 2

Now, to free his mind of any thoughts, speak softly as you give
him the following instructions: "Picture a place inside your
head, just above the top of your nose and between your eyes.
Imagine there's a big, white screen in this special place."

Step 3

Ask your child to concentrate on the blank screen and think of
something from one of the stories in this book, perhaps
the beautiful hummingbird in "The Red Trumpet Flowers".
Invite him to imagine this bird as you describe it. For example:
"It's a tiny, shiny bird, all the colours of the rainbow, with
shimmering wings." Develop his visualization by asking him to
imagine the bird's movements as the story progresses, like this:

Step 4

"Imagine this bird as it hovers beside a big red flower that looks
like a little red trumpet. It beats its silvery wings so fast that you
can barely see them at all. Now the bird sticks its long bill down
the trumpet flower and sucks up the flower's sweet nectar."

Step 5

"Now imagine the tiny bird leaving the red flower. Watch as she
flies above the treetops, dancing, spinning and twirling through
the air. Now the bird has gone and you can't see her any more."

Step 6

Finally you can say: "Let the hummingbird fade completely
from your mind. Notice that the screen between your eyes
is empty and it's time to focus on the peaceful and
comforting empty space the bird has left behind."

A Rabbit to Cuddle

Most children like animals, especially baby ones. Animals often make them feel happy and secure, loved and wanted. This visualization will give them comfort if they're anxious and it will probably make them smile, too! Gently speak these words, pausing briefly at the end of each sentence:

"Imagine you're walking across a field. As you walk, you feel the spiky grass tickling your bare ankles. Suddenly, a baby rabbit appears in front of you. You kneel down to look at him, and he hops into your arms. Now imagine what this cuddly little rabbit feels like. Is he soft and silky or smooth and velvety? Notice the fluffy brown fur on his back and his pure white tummy. He has a little round tail and long, smooth, floppy ears. The baby rabbit looks up at you with his big, brown eyes. He twitches his nose, as if to smell you, and his long, hairy whiskers twitch, too. He seems to like you. And you like him as well, so you give him a cuddle. Now the baby rabbit jumps down from your arms and starts hopping across the field once again. Quickly, you follow behind him. Just then, two more, bigger rabbits appear and start hopping beside you. They're the baby rabbit's mother and father. Soon you're running through the grass with three fluffy rabbits. You start to smile . . . you start to laugh. The baby rabbit has made you feel happy, cheerful and calm."

137

The Watchful Horse

Many people find that their most creative and original ideas come to them when their minds are relaxed and open. This visualization not only encourages creativity, but also introduces the concept that our moods change, depending on events. You might say something like this:

"Imagine a horse grazing on juicy, green grass. Notice her sleek black colour, how she swishes her long tail from side to side, and the way she's standing — with the weight taken off one of her hind legs. Look at the contented expression on her long face — with her droopy top lip, her ears that hang loosely to the sides, and her eyes, soft and dreamy. You can see she's relaxed. But now a barking dog startles the horse and she looks more alert. She pricks up her ears and her eyes look much brighter. Her lip starts to quiver as she snorts through her flared nose. You can see that she's scared. The barking dog runs closer. The horse tilts back her head and her ears lie flat on her neck. She wrinkles her nose, shows the whites of her eyes and bares her big teeth. You can see that she's cross. The dog runs away and the horse is calmer again. Her ears twitch a little. Then she hangs her head low. Her eyelids and lips are all droopy. She takes the weight off one hind leg. You can see she's relaxed, but you know she's aware of the things all around her."

As Tall as a Tree

This visualization gives children the chance to imagine themselves as tall and strong — as being as proud and courageous as any of their friends, and able to do whatever anyone else can do. It will also help to build their self-confidence and give them a positive self-image. You might say this:

"Imagine you're the tallest, strongest tree in the world. Think about your long, sturdy roots that grow deep into the ground. These roots hold you upright, and keep you steady and firm. Nothing can move you from where you are rooted. Now picture in your mind the solid, broad trunk of this proud tree, covered in thick, knobbly bark that protects you from harm. Imagine, your trunk divides high above the ground into branches that seem to reach for the sky. Birds flutter in and out of your branches and the sun glimmers through your bright leaves. And, once again, you have a powerful sensation that you are the tallest and strongest tree in the world. With your head high in the air, you stand firm and steady. How does this feel? Imagine you're growing even taller, so tall that your head — the very top of the tree — is close to the clouds. You see other trees far below you. But none are as tall as you. As your branches sway gently in the wind, strength and courage flow through you, and you know that you can do whatever you wish to do."

Index of Values and Issues

These two complementary indexes cover the specific topics that the 20 stories of this book are designed to address directly or by implication. The same topics are covered from two different perspectives: positive (Values) and negative (Issues). Each index reference consists of an abbreviated story title, followed by the page number on which the story begins.

Acknowledgments

The Publishers would like to thank the four storytellers for
writing the stories listed below:

Anne Civardi:

The Red Trumpet Flowers,

Granny Dean's New Home,

A Curious Kangaroo

Joyce Dunbar:

The Shadow Child,

The Lovable Monster,

The Rainbow Cat,

The Magic Meadow,

Dancing with Moon Sprites

Kate Petty:

The Helpful Fox,

Bubbles of Laughter,

Something to Smile About,

The Mud Man,

Oodles of Oobles

Karen Wallace:

The Star Catchers,

Home to Penguin Island,

A Sheep's Best Song,

An Alligator's Good Friends,

An Elf's Tale,

A Bed for Winter,

The Monkey King